CIBN CONNECT TESTIMONIALS

Hello! If Kerry is not on the top of your "Business Trainers" and "Professional Business Networking Professionals, Leaders, and Trainers," lists, you really need to fix that! Wow! Her brain never stops as she designs additional ways to benefit those she serves. As an example of her expertise, after a short conversation with her, one of my colleagues brought in a multiple six figure increase within the next six months. Do you see why I say, "Wow!

- Wendy Kraft Raleigh, North Carolina USA

Kerry George is more than one-in-a-million, as many, including me, will happily offer with glowing reviews and multiple examples of how she has successfully up-leveled the lives of countless entrepreneurs. She is, in fact, a once-in-a-lifetime discovery.

There is no one with Kerry's level of talent, passion, networking brilliance, business acumen, and energetic personality. She has a sense of humor and wit about her that is truly magnetic. Kerry's faith in you and what you want to accomplish in life is, indeed, life changing. Since you only have this one life, I offer the highest recommendation for you connect & collaborate with Kerry George NOW.

- Tif Loeffler St.Paul, Minnesota USA

I recommend Kerry George for her exceptional entrepreneurial skills, networking business acumen, and ability to connect people. She has a proven track record of success in launching and growing businesses and is passionate about mentoring and coaching aspiring entrepreneurs. She is a true asset to any organization looking to grow and navigate today's challenging environments.

- Greg Belanger, Calgary, Alberta CANADA

Working with Kerry behind the scenes, I have seen how brilliant she is in business strategy and networking. Her compassion for others, integrity, and management skills are first class. Wrap that up with high energy and her big smile you have a winning combination. I appreciate the opportunity to work with her and would not hesitate to recommend her and CIBN Connect as the way to grow your business.

- Cheryl Erickson, Milk River, Alberta CANADA

Kerry George provides an amazing resource through CIBN Connect for businesses of all types to grow together through networking, referrals, masterminds and training. Kerry is a masterful marketer who cares deeply about increasing the success of her members.

- Sheyenne Kreamer, Raleigh, North Carolina USA

Kerry has built an incredible community of entrepreneurs supporting each other to grow their business through referrals. It's not just another networking group. Kerry generously shares her knowledge of creatively getting more leads through networking and social media. Thanks for all your support!

- Nikki Chang-Powless, Calgary, Alberta CANADA

If you want to truly understand why you need consistent business networking for your business and how it will positively impact you then a conversation with Kerry is a must! Her knowledge and understanding of how to effectively network with other business owners to increase your business are immense. As the CEO of CIBN Kerry provides as much support as members could ask for as she believes in helping them achieve success. Kerry and the CIBN have been an important part of my success since June 2016.

- Keith Uthe, Calgary Alberta CANADA

Kerry continues to be one of my suppliers/ mentors in the marketing and networking part of my business. The lady is AMAZING!! Her grasp of what works and is effective in the social media realm is truly cool. She has helped me gain traction where I had nothing but ice under the tires! CIBN Connect has been a great success for me! I can't say enough about the great attitude and caring nature of Kerry!

- Allan MacDonald, Sudbury Ontario CANADA

Why are you reading this!? You probably ALREADY know Kerry! EVERYBODY knows Kerry!!! Kerry George is a force to be reckoned with - the quintessential people and idea connector. Across Alberta and beyond, she is relied on by smart professionals from varied industries for doing something she clearly loves doing and excels at...-almost like she's having a little too much fun! Doing business with Kerry essentially translates into the blah being elevated to the profound...-with giggles thrown in! Let her take your business, and its real-life and online networking associations to new and stratospheric altitudes and laugh all the way to the bank!

- Coral Francis-Callender, Calgary Alberta CANADA

SMART NETWORKING

The $150,000 Method

KERRY GEORGE

An amateur networker is hoping to meet the exact right person in the event. The professional networker knows his exact target is not in the room, ever. He is instead looking to meet and win over the person who knows his ideal client.

~Kerry George

SMART
NETWORKING

The $150,000 Method

**POWERFUL LESSONS
FOR A PROFITABLE BUSINESS**

Kerry George

SMART NETWORKING THE 150,000 METHOD
By Kerry George
Published by Scroll Publishing Inc

Disclaimer: The purpose of this work is to educate and provide mental nourishment. Neither the author nor the publisher shall have any responsibility or liability to any person or entity with respect to any loss or damage caused, or alleged to have been caused, directly or indirectly by the information contained in this book.

The concepts and strategies contained herein may not be suitable for your situations. The ideas and the information shared herein are solely for the purpose of sharing information about the topic presented. This information is intended to complement other information in this field, not to provide an all-inclusive body of knowledge on the topic. Readers are urged to read as much as possible about this topic and to tailor this information to meet their own needs.

The author of this book encourages readers to share the knowledge and insights gained from its contents with others, fostering a culture of personal growth and well-being. Permission is hereby granted to readers to share or quote reasonable sections of this book for non-commercial purposes, provided proper attribution is given to the author.

Fonts: Lucida Fax and Georgia
ISBN No. 978-0-9881297-3-3

TABLE OF CONTENTS

Most people make sales by winging it, but winging it is for KFC or for beer and wings night at the bar. Winging it is not a sales process.

~Kerry George

CHAPTER ONE

WHAT I LEARNED WHILE DOING IT WRONG

Once upon a time in a land far away there was a single mother of three children who could not seem to do anything right. She tried different vocations and then decided to start a business. Again, she did most things wrong, but she figured out one thing, and that one thing gave her a future and a hope. That one thing was networking, and it was networking that changed everything. This is where our story began, and it is where your story can start anew.

For the first forty years of my life, the mistakes that I made were my teachers. I made a mistake and learned from it, and then I made another mistake and learned again. Then something amazing happened. I found mentors who spoke into my life, and I had a revelation. I began to learn from them instead of making mistakes. Overall, having mentors, coaches and like-minded people in my life has been a huge time-saving strategy and learning opportunity, and I highly recommend incorporating this approach into your life.

When I began my networking journey, I was a brand-new business owner and I needed to get my business in front of other businesses so they would buy my services. At the time, I was selling online marketing. I made Facebook backdrops, and I wrote content for email marketing.

Today that seems like a no brainer. Every business owner understands they need to do at least some online marketing. When I entered this industry, nobody really understood what online marketing was. My method of getting new clients was literally aimed at trying to kick down the doors of corporations that were in my city. These were primarily oil and gas companies, and I would try to get appointments booked with top executives so I could explain to them their need for expanding into this new online presence in the marketplace. Most showed me the door. They said it was a fad and it would go away. They said they already had a website, and they certainly did not need to engage in any social media or Facebook hype. I was often invited into a boardroom full of old men and told that I had to use a flip chart for my presentation because they did not have a method of connecting my laptop to a television screen.

GETTING INVOLVED IN IN-PERSON NETWORKING

A friend invited me to an in-person networking meeting filled with small business owners. We were each given only one minute to introduce ourselves. I do not remember what I said in that minute, but it must have been impressive because I was later surrounded by entrepreneurs and salespeople who were eager to hear everything I had to say about this new way of marketing. I was immediately invited to speak at a future meeting, and over the next few months my marketing business began to blossom through attending networking meetings.

Fortunately for me, one of the organisers of a business group took a special interest in helping me learn how these networking meetings ran. Running a networking organisation involves WORK in capital letters and he was desperate to have help. He was incredibly good at bringing people together, nurturing them and making them feel like they were part of a community, but he was horrible at marketing. With knowing how to promote the events and how to add training for the entrepreneurs using my teaching skills, the group began to grow dramatically. I was happy I was getting more business. Networking was proving to be a winning strategy for my bottom line.

Imagine my horror one night when he called to tell me he wanted to retire and spend more time in Florida. He was going to shut the group down. At that point, I had made over $80,000 from that one group alone; it was the only thing that was working for me. Obviously, I did not want him to close it, so I decided I would take over the group. That was the day the empire began.

BECOMING A NETWORKING LEADER

Over the next year, I built out the Calgary Business Network. At the time, most of the networking meetings were monthly meetings and they took place in four separate geographic sectors in this city of a million people. I put together a more valuable offering and we began charging membership fees. I used my organic marketing skills making posts on Twitter and LinkedIn to bring more people to the in-person events. Within months, I had thousands of local businesspeople following us on our social media channels. My marketing system was working well and within one year this second business was making a profit.

All this activity brought us to the attention of our largest competitor who then approached me and asked if I would like to buy his business. It was an intriguing idea. I immediately saw the value of being at the helm of a larger network. Being the leader of a large networking group like this could give me a larger measure of respect in the community. I also felt it could be the platform I was looking for to grow my online marketing business. But with the takeover would come challenges I would need to overcome. When I had started, I was a broke single-parent mom with three children. Things had gotten better since I started my own business, but I was still not flush with cash. There was a large ticket price on this opportunity and the culture of this network was different than the culture of the network I had been building. I knew that going in. I knew it was going to be a lot of work.

I asked tough questions before I decided to move forward, but I did not ask the right questions. In the due diligence process, I did not really know how to do the diligence. I was new to the business world. I did ask for demographics, and I did ask for the proof of the money they said they were bringing in. I was handed a book of documents that was about an inch thick, but I did not know how to read those documents. I did not know that I should be looking at things like cash flow. I did not know that I should ask questions about the cost of the acquisition of a lead, or what the profit margin was? I did not ask about expenses. I was just networking, and I was having fun so I thought this expansion would simply mean it would be more fun. I was good at networking so how could this be any different than just going to a networking meeting and getting clients for my online business?

I thought back to my early days of going to business networking meetings. I had once attended an event put on by the organisation that was approaching me now and I had not enjoyed it. It was not enough, however, to alter my romantic point of view when it comes to networking. Building relationships is emotional and has a lure about it. Are you familiar with the kind of woman who meets a man and thinks he has so much potential that she can change him to be the kind of man she wants? Well, that is a lot of work, and it tends not to work out. This is what I was doing with this business decision. I could see a few wrinkles in the suit, but I thought a good ironing would fix it right up. Even though I knew the organization ran regimented meetings that I did not enjoy, I was willing to look the other way and dream about what the meetings could be. At the meetings, people took a turn standing up and delivering an infomercial for one minute. There was only one person per industry, and while that was good for me in my industry, it had the potential of creating problems. From time to time there was a bring-a-guest-to-lunch day and on one occasion I had taken a guest with me. Little did I know it would not be good for my guest. It turns out that I ruffled someone's feathers. At the end of the meeting, she was approached by a member and told she was not welcome because her business impacted on what he did in his business, and he had first dibs. He said she needed to go. Can you imagine being at an event where you paid to attend, and somebody told you at the end of the event that you were not welcome there?

After the event, we were hounded to join their network. The succession of phone calls seemed never-ending. Their approach felt aggressive to me. It was irritating.

They had 17 lunch groups operating in our city as well as groups operating in other cities across Canada. I could see the potential. I had spoken to a number of their members over the last year, and I knew some were not entirely comfortable with the politics associated with the group. Most people said they just wanted to do business and they wanted to have people do business with them. I thought we could easily scrap the political side of the group. The seller wanted to keep running networking meetings with a focus on a particular political bias and I did not see any threat in that. As far as I was concerned that was good news because anyone who was upset with us removing the political element would have a place to go.

My background prior to running a networking group was pastoring. I knew what the numbers were when a new pastor would take over an existing church. Oftentimes, as much as 60% of a congregation will leave with a change of leadership. I did not know much about business, but I assumed that this may be true for taking over a network, too. I felt that I could compensate for this through my strong skills in sales. And, in my mind, I felt encouraged to take on the addition of this group because my son Zechariah had agreed to join me in the venture. He also was a skilled salesperson, and I believed the two of us could make up the loss of members who we expected would leave us within the first twelve months. I did not particularly like the culture of the existing network, but I believed I had a clear path to change the culture to become what we wanted.

If you are starting to get the feeling I was about to bite off more than I could chew, you are right. What I thought was a beautiful ship in the water that was moving towards a clearly defined destination was feeling more like the Titanic with a huge gaping hole in its side. It was leaning heavily into the water, and it was about to sink. I misinterpreted the numbers presented to me and

I had no idea what I was doing. The first year of business saw us experiencing moments of inspiration and fleeting successes along with chaos and disaster but we did persevere.

My estimation that we would lose 60% was correct. We did. However, I was also correct in that my son and I would be able to sell our way out of it. We sold like the wind. We had to. The cavalry was not going to come and save us. We had nothing to fall back on. It was like landing our army on a shore and burning the ships to prevent escape. We simply had to succeed because we would die if we did not.

It was in this journey that we began to learn about what made a network successful, and more importantly what made networking successful for one individual business owner. Our members were not going to pay membership fees every month, month after month, if they were not getting fair value. They needed to be able to get the referrals they were looking for because that was why they were joining our network. Giving them training on social media, or business, or goal setting was just gravy. The networking itself had to be the meat and potatoes.

As we began meeting with the members, we realized that networking often didn't work because they didn't know how to make it work. Business owners, entrepreneurs, and professionals came to networking to get a lead. Often, they were short sighted; they wanted what they wanted right away. They would come to a networking meeting, and they would buy a membership. Then they would expect the leads they needed would immediately flow to them; no other effort on their part should be required.

I had had considerable success networking. I was getting business for my marketing company on a regular basis because of the way I was doing it. In those early years I began to realize that other networkers were not having this success because nobody had mentored them or told them how. They were like the business owner who built a storefront business and thought to themselves, "I have built it; therefore, they will come." They had paid a membership so now everybody was going to give them lots of business, but that is not how it works.

Networking is all about getting somebody to know, like, and trust you so that fellow members will give you a warm introduction to somebody who needs your product or service. Networking is the most cost-effective marketing when practiced properly. It is a waste of time, energy, and money when done ineffectively or wrongly. It is destructive to the entire industry of networking when organizations do not take the time to train their members on how to do it properly.

We go to networking events, and we meet people. Immediately we "like" them, but liking people is not enough. Nobody gives their best client over to a stranger just because we like them. It is natural for us to protect our best client relationships from those that we recently met. We also need to "know" them and "trust" them, if we are going to share our best warmed up leads with them. Knowing and trusting takes time unless we use a guided process with intent. One does not have to wait for this to happen, we can make it happen if we are willing to follow a few proven steps.

There are methods of networking that make the experience very profitable. Professional networkers know these methods and employ them. They make networking look simple. Amateur networkers fail when they hold on to mistaken beliefs and destructive habits coupled with poor skills; they often lack scripted processes. One of the biggest hindrances to their success is their misconceptions about business networking. Here is a list of some I have heard.

COMMON MISCONCEPTIONS ABOUT NETWORKING THAT WILL HOLD YOU BACK:

- Only large networking events are worth while.

- I should use networking to get in front of as many people as possible.

- Free networking is better than paid networking.

- I need to attend a group where people from my exact target market attend the meetings.

- I only want to attend in-person events.

- Networking is only profitable if "the right" people are in the room.

- I should not waste my time with anyone who could not directly do business with me.

- When I give a referral, I should expect one in return.

- We need to be eyeball-to-eyeball or in-person events for networking to work.

- I should not attend the same weekly group where people have heard my presentation before, because they are tired of hearing from me.

- Networking takes too much time.

- Networking costs too much money.

- I am uncomfortable in large groups.

- I do not like public speaking.

- I do not want to talk about myself or my business.

- I never meet anyone interesting at networking events.

- I do not have time for following up the next day after an event.

- Everyone at the networking meeting just wants to sell me something.

- I detest being pitched to.

- I do not want to spend any money to make money.

- I do not like people.

- I hate networking.

In the next few chapters, I am going to show you where these misconceptions have come from, and I am going to show you how to do networking in a way that can be extremely profitable. By my second year of networking, I was bringing in $150,000 a year with my marketing business through networking. If you are not currently bringing in $150,000 a year and you are networking, I recommend you continue to read this book.

CIBN
CONNECT

Want free help for your business?

Go to YouTube and look up CIBN TV

SUBSCRIBE to the channel.

https://bit.ly/CIBNtv

Then visit the playlists for free training on:

How To Increase Revenue by $150,000 (9 Methods)

Social Media Marketing

Sales Help

Networking

Business Growth

And more...

CHAPTER TWO

Buying The Cow

Everybody knows that hundreds of people will give us their free advice and discover it is not worth the paper they would write it on. We all know if something sounds too good to be true, it probably is too good to be true. We suspect that if somebody tries to give us something for free, there must be a catch. So, knowing all that, why would we think we could do free networking and that it would be valuable?

I meet people all the time who think they can go to free networking events and get customers. I challenge them to look at the facts. I ask questions. How many meetings did they attend? How much time did they take driving there and preparing for the meeting? How much time did they spend at the meeting? How much follow up did they do and how many hours did that take? I then ask them to consider how many real appointments ended in sales being made?

The fact is that successful networking takes a particular skill, and we are not going to learn that skill in an organization that does not get paid to do the work of teaching it to us. Think about it. Look for reasons behind the scenes. Why is this free networking in operation? Is the group being run by a real estate agent or a life insurance agent who needs to get more clients? If the person running the group has another business, then this networking could be a side gig. It is not likely to be their current main source of income and that means it may not get their priority time. Is operating a networking group something they do on the side for lead generation for themselves? Even if they have particularly good networking skills and they understand certain things about business, they may not take the time to teach those who attend when they may have another business that divides their time and requires priority regarding their effort and their loyalty.

In 2020, the world changed. Everything went online. People lost their jobs. Thousands had to reinvent themselves. The business coaching industry began to surge because people were looking for something they could do that would create money for them through online meetings. Coaching was not the only industry that saw huge growth. Everyone from engineers to administrative staff decided they could make money from networking. Did you notice a rise in the number of online groups? I watched as some ran their group for free while living off their savings and then tried to monetize the groups in their second year.

PROBLEMS FROM THESE APPROACHES

Firstly, free is never free. Your time has a value. Every hour you spend in the pursuit of a lead needs to be recorded, tracked, and assessed for its value. If we attend an event where we must spend four hours getting a lead and we bill out at $100 an hour, that lead will cost us $400. Therefore, if we are going to take four hours to get that lead, it had better be a high-quality lead, and we had better be guaranteed to get one every time we attend unless, of course, we are getting something of value other than the lead. For example, if we could get some kind of training while we were there, we might utilize that information to increase overall profits in our business. That could be considered an effective use of our time. The point here is that we need to be mindful of the purpose of the event, our purpose for attending the event and the value of our time.

The second problem with using the free approach is that some of these networking organizers have not actually had any real-life experience in business. They are not able to show us how to build out a social media page, or how to create seven hundred pieces of content in seven days for marketing if they have never done it successfully themselves. If they have never run a business before, would you accept their advice on how to grow your business? Any information they might share on the subject could have come from alternate sources such as books or courses. Would you find that of value to you when seeking support to grow your business? Once again, we need to be mindful of the purpose of the event, our purpose for attending the event and the value of our time.

The third problem is a huge problem in networking overall. If we were running a free group, this would take time, so we are going to need volunteers. Guess who gets to volunteer. Even some paid groups operate on volunteerism. For those of us who are entrepreneurs, business owners, or professionals, do we have time to spend three to ten hours a week on somebody else's business? Would we not be better served serving ourselves by investing that time into our own business? Free networking means lots of voluntary work because somebody must do the work that keeps the network going. I have seen how volunteerism wears out business owners and leaves them with less time for creativity or developing their own long term systematic processes for their own business. Volunteerism brings on death to small businesses.

I once heard a very interesting story. I was in my early twenties, and I was listening to a mentor talk about how he had advised a young couple who were living together to get married because they were putting many hours into a business that they were working together. I'm not saying he was right, and I'm not saying he was wrong, but I thought the story was interesting, and I never forgot it. He had told the young man that it would be a good idea for him to marry his partner since they were living together long term and they were clearly planning to build this business long term. Everything seemed to be good in the relationship and so he encouraged him to formalise it. The young man responded with the comment "why should I buy the cow when I can get the milk for free?"

The young man was stating that he was not willing to make a long-term investment in the relationship. It had been free and there were no responsibilities or obligations. It was a distasteful story, but I sometimes remember this story when I'm hearing people talking about getting their networking for free. It reminds me that there is a different perspective at play here. The person feels that they are getting something for free and why should they have to pay for it? But the real problem is not the free networking, it is how they are valuing networking. They think they can get it anywhere, and that it is free or cheap, and it's not worth investing time or money into. But are they making a $150,000 a year from their networking? I am willing to bet, that they're making very little or nothing from their networking experiences. If they are getting anything at all it is just pure luck. It's like licking the crumbs and the scraps off the floor when the banquet table was fully prepared just over their heads. The problem was they wanted to get it for free, so they weren't willing to pay the price of a ticket to eat from the table.

There is a distinctly different perspective at play when networking is free. On the one hand, the person who is getting networking for free thinks they shouldn't have to pay for it. On the other hand, the real problem is not the free networking; it is how they are valuing the networking. They think they can get networking anywhere for free or for cheap, and that networking is not worth personally financing their own marketing endeavour with their own money. But are they making $150,000 a year from their networking? I am willing to bet they are making little from their networking experiences. If they have been there a while, they may have built a few relationships. I have never heard of anyone earning interest on their money without placing it into an interest-bearing vehicle first. To me, networking for free is like that. It is like hoping to earn the interest without making the investment.

Those who offer free networking cause another problem for those of us who do not. It is like living in a city where a job driving a truck is paying $65 an hour, and then there is a massive growth in population with new residents who are suddenly willing to do the work for $8 an hour. Those who run those trucking fleets save big dollars by hiring people who will do the work for less money. Eventually, however, the trucking companies could find themselves paying out more dollars in lawsuits than the $65-an-hour cost of labour would have. The company may find itself paying the price for driving skills that are inadequate by choosing low-cost labour. When free networking is offered to you, it is important to investigate the value of attending the events. Get answers to questions about the things that concern you. How long have they been in business? What is their track record for success? Ask questions. Do your due diligence.

The biggest problem, though, caused by free networking is the mindset it creates. If a person who does not have money wants to stay broke, he should keep himself surrounded by broke people and do everything for free that he can. Training ourselves to get everything that we can without paying for it is going to keep us deeply entrenched in a poverty mindset. We do not begin to grow financially until we start to surround ourselves with people who can mentor us to be something else. Wealthy people simply do not hang out or spend time together at free events. Successful business owners know that marketing has costs.

WHAT'S COFFEE GOT TO DO WITH IT?

When we started our networking business, we began meeting business owners in coffee shops to conduct business. We made a remarkably interesting observation. There were two brands of popular coffee establishments in our city. One brand is widely known across the country as a place where we could get an economical cup of coffee. Let's call it Johnny Thortans. The other brand only serves quality coffee that costs at least five bucks, so we will call that coffee shop Fivebucks. Over the years, even though we realise that those people who drank their coffee at Fivebucks bought our service more often than those who met us at the less expensive alternative, the people who went to Fivebucks had more money to invest in themselves and their businesses. An authentic business owner did not care what the coffee cost. He cared about the experience; he cared about the environment. He wanted a comfortable place to have a conversation with another business owner without interruption. Establishments that carry a higher quality cup of coffee often have a higher quality atmosphere. This point was ever more reinforced to me the more I frequented a particular high quality coffee shop. I found one where the founding principals of some of the largest oil and gas, and tech companies in our part of the world would meet for coffee once a week. They were retired but still highly influential. I realised then that the opportunity to meet someone with this status might be less likely in the venues that had lower prices.

Why is this important? Because we tend to become like the people with whom we hang around. If we are taking steps toward running a successful business and earn a decent income, we are going to need to hang around people who are successful in business.

Once when I was in an extremely low point in my life making little money, it was brought to my attention that if I were to average the income of my five closest friends, that number would tell me what my own income was. I worked out the numbers and found it was exactly true. That was good news because now I knew what to do about my problem. I needed to make new friends, and I found them at networking meetings that had a fee. Once I found my new friends, I met them in beautiful coffee shops with big brown leather chairs and we enjoyed real coffee that came out of a French press, because that is how quality coffee is made.

I remember meeting with one of my early friends in business who had been participating in a free networking group. I had informed her that the owner of the group had asked me to take it over and that I was going to start charging membership fees to attend it. She was horrified. She told me that all the members would leave if we started to charge fees. She said that she would not be able to stay and assist any longer because she could not afford fees. I looked her in the eye, and I asked her, "Do you want me to come down to your level and stay there with you, or should

I take you by the hand and pull you up to a new level?"

I would love to tell you that my friend grabbed my hand and joined me but that is not true. She could not see past the thought of paying a fee. We seldom talked after that and I'm not sure if she's even in business anymore. The learning journey was going to have a cost and she wasn't willing to take that journey. I, on the other hand, invested everything that I had into the journey, and now the journey has taken me to life-changing spaces.

It's Okay To Pay For Marketing

Professionals pay for marketing and marketing of any kind comes with a cost. We can get it cheap, we can get it fast, and we can get it done well...but we only get to pick two out of the three. If we decide that we want it cheap and well done, then we are going to have to use the do-it-yourself method. We will stay up late and give up our family time. That is not cheap. There is a cost to spending time away from our family. We are also deceived about DIY being cheap because the reality is unless we only charge our company $8/hour for whatever service that we provide, our time is not cheap. It has value in real dollars. If we will invoice out at $100 per hour for the service we provide to our regular clients, then every hour we spend online doing our own marketing was costing us $100 per hour. That is what our time is worth. Even if we are spending our late nights doing the work, we run the risk of wearing ourselves out and robbing our clients of our best selves the following day.

If we want cheap and fast, we could buy our leads online, or get 10,000 people to join our X account by buying them. These can be cheap, and they can be fast. But the quality of those leads is going to really suck. Cheap and fast is not a good long-term strategy. Often people can tell when we have purchased followers online because if we are in North America and we bought them online, the chances are that all these followers only speak Chinese or some language other than English. The foreign characters in the writing will show up on the social media page and everyone will be able to tell that those followers are not genuine. The presence of a foreign language will have a cost to the integrity of our business so in the end it's not cheap. In fact, the practice will be expensive because it will tarnish our reputation.

We can buy marketing that will add 100,000 followers on Instagram in a noticeably brief period. We can get thousands to jump into a Facebook group quickly, but this is not cheap. Someone who is just entering the political arena will need a lot of followers on different social media channels with haste. They are competing against somebody who is already in that political spot and who has a massive online following. Can this happen? Absolutely. But this is why a political campaign costs hundreds of thousands or millions of dollars because it takes many Internet elves sitting in quiet rooms pushing buttons to make this happen. It's not cheap. When we buy Facebook or Google ads, it is going to get our stuff out there in front of many connections that we don't currently have, but there is a cost. It's not cheap because it works.

There are no shortcuts when it comes to marketing. There are also no shortcuts when it comes to networking. Networking is one of the least expensive forms of marketing we can have for our business but it's only effective when done correctly. So, let's talk about how to do that.

CIBN
CONNECT

Want marketing help for your business?

CIBN Connect has the tools, the connections,
and tried and true marketing strategies to assist you.

One of our fabulous tools that comes with membership helps
you to book more appointments with qualified and targeted
prospects is our chrome extension. This powerful piece of
software can help you to book up to 20 appointments a week.

Find out more about how to use it,
book time with Joshua and take a tour of the network

https://api.leadconnectorhq.com/widget/groups/bookcibn

Networking weekly with a dynamic group of entrepreneurs will solve every problem that a business owner has.

~Kerry George

CHAPTER THREE

Moving Away From Outdated Traditional Networking

Social media entered the scene decades ago. From that point on, traditional live and in person networking was becoming more and more defunct. This new form of networking now had the ability to become hybrid "social networking" if we married the in-person event with connecting online through channels like LinkedIn or Facebook.

I started thinking about that in 2015 but I felt hindered by the old boy's club that wasn't willing to transition away from an ineffective and outdated model. The pandemic shifted the way the entrepreneur thought about networking. Business could not afford to be on hold while public gatherings were on hold. Could business still be conducted by members building relationships in online networking meetings instead of brick-and-mortar events? I thought so. It was time to give traditional networking a proper burial and move on to things that actually worked. It was time to start a networking revolution and disrupt the current system with something far more effective.

It was 2011 when I started my own personal networking journey. Like most business owners, all I wanted was a warmed-up lead so I could get business. I would go to the in-person networking meetings, find people who wanted my services and engage others who were willing to refer their clients to me.

Most networking meetings I attended allowed only one person per industry. In the beginning, it was easy for me to be that one person because the whole online marketing scene was brand new. It did not take long, though, for that industry to become flooded. Suddenly there were long lineups of people like me wanting to get into the same club. In the traditional model, fifteen of us would be interviewed but only one would be chosen to fill the vacant spot. Usually, we would be the one selected if we had been in business the longest, and if they felt that we had a network of people who we could potentially refer to their networking organization.

I found the logic of this to be faulty. I quickly realized the most professional and longest-term real estate agents and life insurance agents in the group came into the networking community with a network of their own already. They had a previous long-established relationship with a mortgage broker to whom they referred people, so they weren't willing to refer people to the mortgage broker that was in their new networking club like they were supposed to do. These clubs often had penalties for not giving a lead that week so they would get into the habit of referring their sister-in-law to everybody in the room. I am certain that woman had no idea why all these people were calling her.

By 2012, I was running my own business network. I had found there was a more effective way for getting quality warmed-up leads and I was able to impact the other members of the group by training them to be more efficient. I had another advantage over most business owners and that was that my background was in online marketing. Soon I began offering training to the members so they could become effective in this, too.

We added training that taught people how to give ten referrals to somebody they had met only a short time ago and then we added training on how to receive ten referrals from other members of the group. We stopped giving penalties to those who didn't have a lead because it only led to members giving bogus leads. We wanted the leads to be authentic and genuine and making this change alone resulted in a significant difference in the outcome. The closing ratio from a quality lead given in a warmed-up email where the three parties are all in the same message can be expected to yield a 50% return ratio even if the receiver is a poor salesperson. It's much more effective than saying, "I'll tell my sister-in-law to give you a call."

MERGING THE OLD WITH THE NEW

I quickly began to see that the online networking world needed to merge with the in-person networking world. It made complete sense to me that when somebody went to a networking meeting, they should try to connect with the others at the meeting on social media channels such as LinkedIn. I realized that if you then connected with them on Facebook or Meta, X, Instagram, and other social media channels, they were going to be able to see our posting over and over again. It also made sense to me that if I met a person on a social channel, the next step should be to invite them to my networking meeting. In fact, if I targeted the exact industry that would do business with me on LinkedIn and then invited those who responded to my next networking meeting, they could get to know me. If they became a member, they would see me every week and I could pitch to them repeatedly. It was a significantly beneficial use of my time and a winning marketing strategy.

During this time, it was widely accepted in the sales arena that it would take seven to fourteen touches or points of contact with a prospect to get a sale. Therefore, if I were meeting somebody for the first time and they said "no" to buying my services, I would want to get them into my personal social media vortex. That way, they would see things I was posting and things I was saying, and they would feel like they were being touched by me in an automated way, even though I was not there personally talking to them. I began to develop the system of doing this and teaching it to others who are part of my networking group. This collaboration became highly effective but not everybody was open minded to adding these new forms of social networking to their existing networking methods.

By the year 2015, I was already thinking that networking with business owners could be done more efficiently if we did it online using a tool like Zoom. When I brought this idea to members of my organization, I was met with immediate resistance. I was that I must be "eyeball-to-eyeball" for networking to work because people need to get to know, like and trust each other in person and they would not do that through online meeting spaces. Some even went as far as to say you had to be "belly-to-belly" whatever that means. I told them to keep their belly away from mine!

I understood there were two things that business owners continuously struggled with. These were a lack of money and a lack of time. Business owners were always trying to overcompensate for these things by making more money and increasing their bottom line, but the ongoing problems were always around money and time, not just money.

I could see that the way we were doing traditional networking was sucking up money and time. It could take an hour to drive across town and find parking. Then we would go into the networking meeting and oftentimes volunteerism would be involved. After we set up the meeting and participated in the meeting, we did not have much time left to talk to people individually. At some meetings, we only had time to talk to the person who sat next to us to the right and the person on the left during the meal. We sometimes had a one-on-one on site before going out to our car and driving back across town to our office. We would have a stack of business cards in our hand that would take an hour of follow-up on the phone the next day just to get a couple of those people to book appointments. Overall, if attending one meeting was consuming five hours or more of our time, this was an inefficient use of our time and our money. Doing business this way has been a drain on small business owners for decades.

I was not afraid of the Internet because I used it every day in my first business as an online marketer. In my mind, it would be more efficient and effective to pop into a Zoom meeting and finish the entire event within one hour. I could see the possible timesaving hacks like "booking a meeting from the meeting while you're in the meeting" so you do not have to make the follow-up calls the next day. Yet, as I talked to the business owners, they were completely unwilling to change from the method they had become accustomed to.

Their reluctance to shift made me curious about the history of networking. Why were these intelligent entrepreneurs convinced they needed to be face-to-face to be doing networking? I could see that some of the hesitancy was coming from loyalty to established models they had experienced themselves, but I soon discovered much of this was coming from ancient times.

THE HISTORICALLY OF NETWORKING

Networking is not new. It is likely as old as humanity itself. I can imagine a time thousands of years ago when there was some guy named Dave who lived in a cave, and he was selling bone sharpeners. He had a friend named Peter who lived down by the water and sold fish. Whenever somebody would buy one of Dave's bone sharpeners, he would tell them they could get good fish from his friend, Pete, down on the beach.

As trade developed between different peoples, networking became a method of increasing business. Merchants would travel along the silk road between the Orient and Europe, and they would bring with them their spices and their silks and other popular products. When one merchant would get the business of a local king, he often would recommend one of his fellow merchants who was traveling with him in the caravan. These sellers of goods would travel together because they were able to have more protection when they went in a group. Marauders and thieves would frequent the roads and sometimes sweep down from the hills and steal the wares of the merchants. They found when they worked together, they could protect one another. Many of our networking practices were born during these times and even today members of a business network will watch out for one another.

Every castle in Europe had an economic trade center. Merchant guilds emerged in these feudal systems. They would have a butcher, a baker and a candlestick maker and they would all look out for one another. If somebody came into town who hadn't paid his bill to one of them, they would let the others know this somebody was not trustworthy. They also found if they got together, they had more power with the local authorities. If the king decided one day that he didn't like the food the baker was making, he could fire him or behead him and send out a decree for a new baker. However, when the merchants of the guild worked together, they became an advocacy group. The king did not necessarily want to start chopping off one guy's head if there was going to be a bunch of people saying, "I'm not going to serve you anymore." Suddenly, the guild had power because no kingdom could survive without the meat from the butcher, and it would be a dark place if the candlestick maker stopped making his candles. These guilds were the first networking groups and they looked very much like the networking groups we are still experiencing in the 21st century.

One more recent communication device before the Internet arrived was the business card. History tells us the first ones originated in China. By the 18th and 19th centuries, business cards were being used in France and England, and then later across Europe and North America as calling cards. By the 21st century print shops were designing and printing business cards for business owners on a regular basis. Many of us who went out to in-person events would collect boxes of business cards, and many of us would not do anything further with them. We had a box museum somewhere in our office where business cards went to die a slow death in hiding.

NETWORKING IN THE 21ST CENTURY

I realized we could use the information on the business cards we collected to create our first email list. The contact information could provide an opportunity for our sales team to invite these people back to networking meetings. We could also invite them to connect with us on LinkedIn. The one thing we needed to do that on LinkedIn in those early years was an email address and that address was on the business cards. By 2015, most business owners were still not doing what we considered to be basic things related to marketing and self-promotion. What I was saying was we could do all this online in a Zoom meeting and they were looking at me like I had two heads. Most were not even connecting on LinkedIn yet.

Where I lived at the time, traditional networking groups had been operating for almost one hundred years. One group in our city was started by members of the business community a century before; some other B2B groups in our area had been founded by members of that original group, so their culture and their methods of operation were quite similar. There was one business owner in each industry category meeting around the table for lunch once a week trying their best to get to know, like and trust each other so they would be comfortable enough to give one another a warmed-up lead. But the constraints of time and money continue to be obstacles to overcome in order to sustain membership in such groups.

Members would not have sufficient time to really get to know one another. One meeting a week was not going to do it. We found that when they followed each other on their social media channels and began to share one another's content back and forth, it increased the feeling that they knew one another better and as a result more warmed-up referrals began to flow naturally through the network. **When we married the old, traditional ways of networking to the new ways of social networking, it**

was much more effective. We discovered that new and modern techniques could be added to the networking process, and these techniques could help business owners increase their bottom line if they were willing to learn the new method.

Traditional networking did not make sense economically. As we were meeting in restaurants or in hotels, these meeting spaces had a monetary cost. We either had to pay for the room and serve coffee with light snacks or we had to purchase meals for everybody at the table so that the commercial enterprise would make their space available to us at no cost. The cost of food for our network in this one city was $180,000 a year. That cost needed to be passed down to the end user who was buying a membership for $700 up front and then paying a monthly fee which covered the cost of the food. This was expensive networking.

My business coach joked one day that I was feeding more people in our city than the food bank was. We could get rid of the cost of food if we could just convince people that online was a better method than doing it live and in person. This would make it better for everyone.

Traditional networking was becoming increasingly more challenging. it was running its course and new methods were coming straight at us. I wanted to be the disruptor at the beginning of that curve and not the late adopter at the end of that curve. I could see that if we met online in a Zoom meeting, we would be able to completely cut out the cost of food.

THE MOVE TO ONLINE NETWORKING

By 2017 we had put our video portal together where we had recorded many of the training sessions we had done on subjects like networking, social media training, content writing, goal setting, and general knowledge about how to grow business. In the Spring of 2019, we opened our first online networking groups using Zoom. We began rewriting our automated systems for an online network. We rebranded our Canadian company into a global organization. By January 2020 we had a new logo and a brand-new website. Our latest sales and training material was ready to launch a major worldwide initiative. Now we just had to convince our tribe that this was the right decision.

When March 2020 arrived and the pandemic happened, we were poised and prepared for what came next. We took our in-person groups and moved them online in less than 24 hours on March 13th. And it was business as usual for our networking organization. Everybody went to their computers and followed through with their networking just like they would if they were going to a meeting at the restaurant.

At this point we had a full year of data showing us that people could network online, and, in fact, it was less than one quarter of the cost and it took less than one quarter of the time. Furthermore, the average networker was bringing in three to four times the profit than they did in the traditional model.

The biggest problem was that some members did not like it. It did not feel like networking to them because they were not sitting across the table from each other over a meal. I remember having a conversation with a business coach who told me that in-person networking was the only way to go. So, I asked him as a business coach if his client would come up with a way to do something for one quarter of the cost and one quarter of the time and it brought in three times the profit, what would he tell his client? He immediately responded that he would, of course, tell his client that the new method was a better method. I then told him that was the difference between networking in the traditional, face-to-face model versus networking online. He then admitted that a good business coach would be telling his clients to do more online networking. Comically, however, he went on to say he was not that good business coach. He admitted he would let his emotions rule his own decisions and keep getting the weaker results.

Between March 2020 and the spring of 2022, I listened to members of the original group from our city continuously talk about the loss of friendships and the loss of relationships and the loss of opportunities due to going online. At the same time, however, we saw hundreds of new people join our organization from across the globe. As they came in with a fresh perspective and a different attitude, it positively impacted their results. They reported that networking online with our organization was changing the way they did business. They were learning how to do things online and how to market themselves in ways they had never dreamed, hoped, or imagined. They reported increases in profit, and they often shared they had new friends from across their country and across the world with whom they felt connected just as if they had met them in person. I personally know of several who have forged longstanding relationships which have continued to this day. I expect they may have become life-long friends.

The only difference between these two groups of people was their perspective. This is often the case in life. Is our glass half empty? Or is our glass half full? Henry Ford said it best with, "If we believe we can, we can, and if we believe we can't, we can't."

I believe we can.

For more than a decade we met with people at in-person events face-to-face. We became so effective at networking and helping the business owners in our organization succeed that we went years without losing a single member to business failure. In a world where 80% of businesses fail in their first five years and 90% of businesses fail in their first ten years that is a remarkable claim. I knew by 2015 that we needed to take this message to the world.

Traditional networking is old and outdated and there is a better way of doing it. There is so much more we can offer to the business community than just getting together to see if we can wrangle a lead out of each other. The method of having one person per industry around a table is no longer necessary. When we have an attitude of abundance and collaboration, we don't need to be tied down by beliefs that our competition should be excluded from the conversation. That belief sets up limitations. When abundance thinking is embraced by us as entrepreneurs, we are open to discover there is more than enough business in the world for us all; we get more when we give more.

When I purchased that "old boy's club" in an oil and gas city in 2013, we had more than 95% men in the group. More than 80% of those men were over the age of 55. If I had done my homework better, I doubt I would have bought it. But we learned from this experience, and we changed the culture of the group. Within a few short years, our membership had grown to being 40% women and today we have 60% women across our network. Apparently, having a strong female leader attracts female leaders. Today we are a mixed bag of colors, genders, cultures, and religious denominations. We are building a modern business organization that is for entrepreneurs, business owners, and professionals from diverse sectors who want to succeed. These are the backbone of our society. These people create the numbers in support of our gross domestic product. Small businesses employ more people than large corporations in every country on Earth and effective networking helps them to win in every area of their lives and their businesses.

Modern networking uses online methods to talk to people and build relationships. Where possible, it combines the online world with brick-and-mortar and in-person events. Everything else is not only old fashioned, but also a waste of time.

There is one long-standing reason people are trying to hold onto the old ways. It is because to some it feels good; it is what they know. They are comfortable there. It's like wearing a favourite pair of well-worn slippers. The slippers, however, are ugly and old. They are no longer adequate. It is time to move on. It is time to let go of the old and embrace the new.

If we have been around the business world for a while, we come to learn that running a business by our feelings does not tend to be effective. Imagine if we stopped trying to sell a product because our friend made a negative comment about it. Getting wounded and sucking our thumb in a corner will not produce sales. Seasoned entrepreneurs know this. They know that genuine business owners make decisions based on data. They look at trends and they see how the market is responding.

The data is in. Doing traditional networking alone is on its way out just like the fax machine. There is a new ride-share service in town, and it is faster and cheaper and more effective than calling a taxi.

I hope to see you at a networking meeting soon on Zoom or in whatever online platform that comes next. The world is changing, and we are changing with it.

Visit the CIBN Connect event page at https://cibnconnect.com/ cibn-events

To see modern networking done right check out the CIBN Connect events

CHAPTER FOUR

What Is Networking Worth?

Have you ever heard that what we think about the most is what we become? Has someone ever told you what we focus on is what is drawn to us? That is what I think most people have learned about the law of attraction and I think most people believe what comes around goes around to some extent at least. How might this ability to attract what plays out in our mind affect us in our networking?

We all have attitudes, beliefs, and ways of being based on our experiences and our training. We are the compilation of the people we hang around with, the things we have read, and the courses we have taken. How much of that time did we spend trying to figure out how to network more effectively?

Practice Helps

It is fair to say it takes about 10,000 hours to become a professional at anything. If we want to be comfortable standing and speaking on a public stage in front of masses of people, it might require starting with practice standing on a stage in front of more than one person. If we want to master playing an instrument, we may simply have to spend more time at it. Why would networking be any different?

Many business owners who go out networking for the first time suck at it. They may feel overwhelmed and out of place and look like they don't enjoy talking to strangers. They may feel uncomfortable standing up in front of a group of people talking about themselves and their business for even a single minute. If they don't receive business from the exercise immediately, they start to feel like networking this way is an ineffective use of their time, and as these opinions begin to solidify, they take root in the subconscious mind. What follows is the silent stories in our head that lead to self-sabotaging any possibility for success.

The fact is that somebody in our industry is making money from networking. Now why shouldn't that somebody be us?

What is keeping us from making $150,000 a year in our chosen business from networking? It could be that we don't know the methods that work. It may also be that we lack practice. Or it may be that we have formed opinions and attitudes that are working against us.

As to methods, you will find tried-and-true networking methods as you continue to read this book. As to the issue of practicing networking, get out there and practice. Do it in person. Do it online. And as to what you are telling yourself, that is a head game that takes place in the distance between your ears...about 15 centimetres or six inches. It may the toughest six inches you will ever trave to overcome self-doubt and negative thoughts.

If we think that networking is fun and that business comes to us easily through the process of networking, then we are going to have amazing and impressive experiences every time we go networking. If we think that networking is demanding work, and that nobody understands what I am saying, and it never leads to anything good, then networking is going to suck. So, I would ask myself, "How do I feel about networking?"

EMOTIONS AND MINDSET PLAY A PART

Did you know that when we identify how we feel about something, and we are aware of the emotions erupting inside us, we will become empowered to do something about it. That means if we know something would be good for us, then we can decide to accept that and take the first steps toward a productive end. If our networking experiences in the past have been less than stellar, now would be an optimum time to acknowledge that. Can we put our finger on exactly what made us feel that way? Was it one of the things I already mentioned? Can you see how the results might be different if the mindset was different?

Let's open the mind and start thinking about ways to make this work instead of ways that it doesn't work. The mind is like a parachute: it works best when it is open.

These are some common misconceptions about networking that may be influencing how we think about networking:

- Networking needs a large group of people present.

- The right person must be in the room.

- These people are not worthy of my time if they don't have the money to buy my thing.

- I have better things to do.

- I am no good at it.

- This is so hard.

Do Numbers Matter?

In our early years of running a networking organization, we had a small group of eight people who consistently met every week for lunch. We ran a survey of how our business owners were doing. We wanted to know how many leads they were getting and how much new business each group was bringing in. The results of this small group were surprising.

We got the idea from one of our competitors because they were putting an individually set price tag on the industry seat, and they had only one person in each industry who could occupy that seat. They were basing that price on how many dollars were generated for the business by the overall group. I was suspicious of this. Was it a faulty presumption? I had discovered that their method for bringing new members into their group was to interview several people for the same position. They then picked who they thought would be the highest producer. So, for example, if I was going to invite a real estate agent to join the group in this outdated model, I would first interview 15 real estate agents and try to pick the one who had the highest sales ability and the largest existing network assuming they would be able to bring more people to our club because of their existing relationships.

There were so many problems with this model. Firstly, the successful candidate came in with elevated expectations of what this group was going to do for them, instead of asking, "What value could I bring to this group?"

High producers often arrived with this sense of entitlement. If I brought in a high producing real estate agent and he only received five warm leads this year, the chances were good he was going to close four out of the five. Since the price of housing in our community runs between $500,000 and a million dollars per unit, that means I am going to be able to brag that our club did over two million dollars worth of volume and that number would be based primarily on what the real estate agent did. If I use the same method of recruitment for the life insurance category, the web designer category, the mortgage broker category, and the accounting category, we could have high numbers in this club. We would be able to say that the club did exceptionally well, and that the overall revenue brought in by the members for the members was outstanding. What about the network marketer though? What about the lady who owns a flower shop?

The retention rate in this kind of organization is around 28%. This is because the little guy doesn't make a lot of money and he puts in a lot of volunteer time. The numbers derived from the big-ticket sales are not the numbers that should matter. The little guys matter too. They need the networking to work more than any of the big players because they will not be in business next year if it does not work. Networking done well would save their business. If the networking support model does not include being shown a successful path by its leaders, members will leave the group and become networking refugees. Entrepreneurs who have tried networking and found it lacking are out there. They are wandering the earth feeling forsaken and believing that networking was a big waste of their time. Nobody ever explains to them that the model was wrong. Therefore, they believe they are no good at it, or that networking itself is at fault.

Wouldn't it be better if everyone in the group was there because they needed the business? That would mean if I were currently going to the grocery store buying popular name-brand products, I should be willing to try out the network marketer's product which could be delivered for a competitive price right to my door. That would mean if I had a second cousin who's a real estate agent, I am now going to use the real estate agent in my club because that person has committed money and time to be in part of the same organization as me; I want to give him my preferred business so he will give me his preferred business. What if I have been going to the same accountant for years? Has he ever given me a lead? Has he ever been to my house for dinner? If not, why should I keep giving him my business when there is an accountant sitting here in the room with me who needs my business? If everybody in the room is eager to give business to one another and they are eager to use each other's services, then it will not take long for them to eagerly refer their best clientele to one another. In this supportive environment, there is a potential for a lot of leads to go around. This is a happy and winning club. Does it matter if the club did two million dollars worth of revenue as a whole? Shouldn't it matter more that everybody in the room got business?

Stacking the deck with the most successful salespeople is not what is best for the small business owner in the room. It is best if we use each other's services and if we genuinely care about one another.

There is all this talk about getting to know, like and trust one another. What if it wasn't just talk? Wouldn't that be cool?

One of our competitors was highly effective at bringing a sizable number of business owners together for a meeting. It was a standard practice in the networking industry that we needed to have a group of 25 to 40 members so there would be a respectable number of referrals given back-and-forth amongst the business owners. They also had regimented rules and embarrassment tactics if one did not comply. Every referral was tracked by the group, and each member was held accountable for giving referrals. The system felt disciplinary to me and not an action I would choose to take in the spirit of doing business and building relationships. We looked long and hard at the model and decided we did not want to be that group.

People are motivated by pleasure or pain and some people do respond better to the stick than they do to the carrot. This model uses the stick. We like the carrot.

We prefer to focus on numbers that, in fact, do matter. Our personal numbers matter. As individual business owners, the group's numbers do not matter to us. Why? Because different people are tracking different things. Price points are also quite different in different product lines. We have met business owners who use a free survey as a lead generator and one of the things they are tracking is the number of free surveys they gave away this month. That is completely different than the guy who is selling a life insurance policy and it is different again from the bakery who is selling coffee and donuts. For a business owner with a large ticket item one sale in the month is more than enough. For another business owner they must sell one thousand small items just to keep the lights on. Adding all our numbers together as a group and claiming we did something great is not as good for us as actual dollars landing in each member's bank account.

There are additional numbers in this model which may never be tracked but worthy of noting. The network marketer might only track the one customer given to her by a member. Does she track the downline of the 50 people who came from that one customer over the next few years? Is the coach who sells a membership service tracking the ongoing revenue that comes from his network? What about the auto-mechanic who learned to use an email list to communicate with his customers from a course he took in the business network? Is he tracking all the business that eventually came from the email list as a positive result of attending the network?

For these reasons and many more, having a big networking group is not necessarily what's going to bring us the big numbers. How many people can we effectively connect with in an hour? I know the number on that. As a professional networker when I am in a live and in-person event, I can only speak with a maximum of 20 people an hour effectively and that is if there is nothing else going on. If the entire hour is dedicated to pure networking without interruptions of speakers and music and all the other things that organizations try to incorporate into the networking event, I can collect 20 business cards and book 20 appointments on the spot. So why would I need to be in a room of 200 people?

I must admit that going into the big networking event makes me feel big and makes me feel important. However, any business coach worth their salt should be telling you that your feelings related to ego are irrelevant. When we make business decisions based on our feelings, we make poor business decisions. The fact is smaller networking groups work better for getting leads because people get to know, like and trust each other at a faster rate when in a smaller group.

What happens in the large group can feel like a one-night stand. It's exciting to be invited into this new group when there are so many people to get around to. The problem is these people do not really know us. Unless you are prepared to commit to building relationships with people you met at this event, these types of activities tend not to produce real and lasting contacts. They produce short-lived good times that are easily forgotten. If you do not believe me, you might think back to a big party you went to in your teens finding yourself swimming in a room of people you didn't know and who didn't notice when you left.

The same is true in business. When we go into a large group, we are not making real relationships that are going to stand out the next morning as being anything special. Everyone in the room collected a heap of business cards and the next day they cannot even remember who those people were. Even when we go into a big online event, the same thing is happening. Everybody is in their own little square box on screen and there's a lot of information going into the chat (if it's a good group that allows you to chat). It all looks exciting, but the problem is we are not making any real relationships happen here and it feels more like a one-night stand.

When people get together in a small group and they see the same people every week, week after week, they get to know, like and trust one another. They become more like family. We care about family, and we want to see them succeed, so we spend time thinking about how we could give them a lead that would impact their ability to feed their children or pay their bills.

Am I In The Right Room?

When we began in the networking industry, we too drank the

Kool-Aid that said every networking meeting had to be a big meeting for it to be successful. We believed this until we had data that said otherwise.

In those original 17 clubs we took over in 2012, a few of them had especially small numbers. One of those groups had only eight members who met every week. We did a survey in the network early on trying to determine which of the clubs produced the most revenue for the members. Imagine our astonishment when we discovered it was this little group. The print and promo guy in that group had been in business for 35 years before he joined our organization. He was upset with us because his business had grown so much. He had been planning to slow down and retire, and now he had to hire fresh staff. The life insurance agent in the group reported more than $30,000 in commissions in the last quarter alone. The realtor and the mortgage broker were happy and closing deals every month in a recessed market. There was a girl selling a network marketing product that took her business to the top in her industry. After two years in that little group, she had made so much money that she left us to travel the world permanently. These were the results in a small group where people cared about each other. And it wasn't just the top producers who were making money, it was everybody in the group.

These people had a great attitude. They believed in themselves and in each other. They enjoyed getting together every week. They spent time thinking about how they could help each other and not just thinking about themselves. They had excellent results. We were so intrigued with these results that we created a networking course based on what they were doing in that club. We still run that training, and we find it is helpful to business owners, entrepreneurs, and professionals to this day.

In networking, the positive attitude we bring to our group is essential for success. In fact, Zig Ziglar is quoted as having said, "Attitude determines altitude."

The beliefs we have often shape our attitude. We have a sense or a gut feeling about what will work, and what won't work, and that has a huge influence on what works for us.

One of the things I hear amateur networkers say all the time is, "The person I'm looking for isn't in this room." If I had a dollar for every time, I heard that, I would be as wealthy as Warren Buffet.

The amateur networker who thinks he must be in the perfect room to get the perfect lead implies there is a room somewhere full of people who are exactly his target market. This is a common misconception held by amateurs and it keeps them from succeeding in their networking. I would love to find that unicorn room somewhere but, truly, it doesn't exist anywhere.

Say for example, that I sell a product to companies that have 20 to 100 employees. I am looking for a company that has a marketing budget of at least $20,000 so they can purchase what I have to offer. I enter a room full of people and find that the average business owner there is making less than a $100,000 a year and they have zero to three employees. If I jump to the conclusion there is nobody in the room who is qualified to buy my product, I am likely to think this is a big waste of my time.

A professional networker understands that the people we are looking for in the room are never in the room. They have already gotten over that notion and they understand that everybody in the room knows people who they did not bring with them. In fact, everybody in the room knows hundreds of people they did not bring with them. A professional networker knows how to connect with those people in the room so he can get them to introduce him to the people he wants to meet and determine if they are qualified buyers for the product or service he offers. For instance, a professional networker will instinctively recognize that the website designer in the room is doing websites for companies which are his target audience and who has direct access to the owner. He will also want to talk to the accountants because the accountants are doing accounting for the companies he wants to get in front of. He knows his relationship with the accountant is extremely important and that it should continue to be nurtured by him over time.

The professional networker never disqualifies anyone in terms of lead generation based on what they do for a living. They understand that everyone knows someone who might offer a connection. The lady who sells Tupperware could be married to somebody who is influential or has a friend who is prominent in the community. The kitchen cabinet maker could be living next door to a neighbour who owns a mobile oil-change service. We will never know unless and until we have the conversation.

We once held a networking meeting where we bought everybody lunch and they got to come for free. We reached out to individuals using LinkedIn and invited them to our favorite Chinese restaurant where we did a one-hour pitch while they ate their lunch. I remember a man who met me at the door when he was leaving telling me in a matter-of-fact way he would not be joining our network. He added that he felt insulted for having been seated next to a lady who sold Tupperware. He did not realize that I intentionally sat him next to her because her husband was an oil and gas executive who was exactly the client this man would need. He completely missed an opportunity because he judged what she did for a living and jumped to the conclusion she could be of no value to him. What a missed opportunity!

This is one example of how our attitude can defeat us. When we believe we know something to be true, we are unwilling to learn anything new. He assumed he knew something and, therefore, missed getting some particularly valuable information. He was arrogant and dismissive to this woman and blew any chance of turning an information-gathering conversation into a productive lead source.

The reality is that the right people are always in the room. Somebody in that room knows the person that we need to meet. What we need to do is win them over

so they will search through their haystack and bring us the one needle that we need.

GIVING AND RECEIVING

Others I have met at networking meetings are tracking how much giving they are doing and creating a scorecard. This is in poor taste. Giving is not giving if we are keeping score.

I should not be counting the number of people I have helped. If I have the expectation that I should get what I give in return, I am in the wrong space, especially if I am thinking I will get business back from that one person I gave a lead to.

It is better to give than to receive. As we give, we should consider the giving as a gift. It should make our heart swell with pride and joy to watch our fellow member get excited over that awesome and perfect lead we just gave to them. We should be eager to send an introductory email to the person we are referring them to and send a CC to the member in the message. We should do it without expectations because gifts should be given without expectations. This is what makes a gift a gift!

A lead is a gift for three people. It's a gift to the member who received the lead. It is a gift to the person with whom we connected them by giving them access to a professional who has a reputation for doing a respectable job and who could save them headaches and stress. It is also a gift for me, the giver. I can experience the thrill and the goodwill of being a giver.

The expectations should not be that the person to whom I gave the lead will make it up to me by giving back to me someday. Instead, the expectation should be that my networking organization will serve me. There will be leads that come from the group. There will be advice that comes from my group and some of that advice will save me thousands of dollars. There may be strategies I learn in this group that will help make me tens of thousands of dollars annually going forward. There will be costly mistakes I get to miss out on because of something I learned or because someone in our network gave good service. There will be skills I learned in the courses I took saving me money because I did not have to pay someone else to do the tasks for me. There will be thousands of dollars made because I hired brilliant people who did an excellent job in a timely manner for a fair price. These are the expectations one should have of their business network, and these are the numbers one should track. How would you like to belong to a business network like this?

Business owners may be advised by their business coaches, accountants, and mentors to track their numbers. When they do, they can calculate their return on investment as it relates to time spent and business gained. That is a fair approach to measuring the value of our time if we consistently track our activity over a sufficient period.

IS SUCCEEDING FASTER POSSIBLE?

Any marketing expert will warn us that it takes months to determine if the fresh marketing plan is working. Networking is a form of marketing. It is like planting a crop, weeding, watering, and then harvesting the crop. There is a season for it. Money does not come pouring out after thirty days. When we join a group, the members need to get to know, like, and trust us. This takes time. It is not realistic if we rush it too much. We have methods that we employ to move the process along at a steady rate, but it is not instant rice. We don't add water and then sprout a relationship!

There are additional factors that feed into the success or failure of the networker's experience. Here is a list of qualities that would aid us in getting faster results:

- We like people.

- We enjoy talking in front of groups.

- We like to learn new things and we have a great attitude about it.

- We have some sales skills so we can close the leads we get.

- We have a sales process and a good follow-up plan.

- We connect with people online after the in-person activity or the online networking event.

- We book a meeting from the meeting every time we are in the meeting.

These things would hinder us and slow down the process:

- Our expectations are wrong.

- Our attitude sucks.

- We do not like people.

- We think we are better than everyone else in the room.

- We hate being in crowds and we don't want to change.

- We are afraid of public speaking, and we resist learning how to overcome that.

- We hate selling and we have no desire to improve our skills at sales.

- We think we know everything and therefore cannot be taught anything new.

- We are bad at networking, and we don't even know it.

The length of time to grow a crop in networking varies according to industry. If I own a coffee shop and I want my fellow members to come in for coffee and use my place as a spot where business owners meet each other, this should not take long to grow a crop. It is likely that a few members will pop by in the first month if they are local to me especially if I give them an incentive to do so such as a coupon for their first cup of java.

Products and services sold by members can range significantly in terms of both quantity and price. Lower-priced items demand larger numbers sold compared to a member who needs to make just one sale in a month or two to score big. Because the problem with smaller offers is that we need more sales, we need a method of tracking data. And we need the numbers to keep stacking up, so they come to a larger number over time. It would be a great idea to use a loyalty card that gets stamped as the member makes repeat returns and there is a benefit to them like a free cup of coffee when they cash in the completed card. Then we could count those cards monthly to see how our loyalty strategy is working. Another possibility is to create a monthly subscription, so the member comes back repeatedly. There could be a tracking code for the member and a separate one for the customers that the member brings to us. These are good business practices for any kind of business. We should know where our business growth is coming from.

If we are looking for big sales where the object or service is greater than $1000, we are going to get fewer leads and it is going to take more time to get them. Nobody is giving us access to their closest friends and best clients to sell them a high-ticket item after having just met us. Who would hand that information over to a stranger? This is a crop that needs a little nurturing. It may take months to get the first sale. A sale combined with a buyer's testimonial could help sales come with more regularity.

IS THE WAIT WORTHWHILE? CONSIDER THESE OUTCOMES.

Years ago, before we started training our networkers to be more effective, we had a realtor who had not made a sale for three years. She came to lunch every week and brought her good attitude with her. She worked on her ability to speak in front of the group. She built relationships. She received help across the different networking skills, but she was not making sales from the group. She almost gave up but then in the beginning of the fourth year she made three sales in the first quarter of the year. By the end of that year, she had made nine sales. More sales came in consistently each year after that. If her average commission was $20,000 and her cost to do networking was about $3000, how did she do?

This same person made other changes, too. She reported that her fear of public speaking was gone. She had saved over $2000 on a roof repair by contracting one of the members. She had developed a system for social media marketing and print marketing that was working for her driving her bottom line up by over 20% per year for four years running. She had learned about investing from one of the financial professionals and had increased her family's net worth by 40% during the same period. She had made good friends with the plumber's wife and another woman who sold cosmetics. She had switched her household purchases to support a healthier alternative and removed toxins from her home while improving the quality of her family's vitamin supplements. She also lost 12 pounds while working with the fitness coach. What was the real value of her business network?

Years ago, we held a meeting where we brought together a few members to explore the subject of bitcoin. One of our members was a single parent mother who was barely scraping by. She was in a direct sales business and not doing that well. She managed to scrape together a few hundred dollars and invested in bitcoin. Last year she withdrew more than $500,000 from her account and bought a house with it. What was the value of her business network?

In 2015 one of our mortgage brokers met another one of the brokers from another one of our clubs. This was a competitor speaking to a competitor about a wealth strategy with a view to helping change lives. They chatted at length about the possibility of owning multiple homes and collecting rent. Over the years we watched this mortgage broker buy several homes and create substantial passive income for himself. He then taught the concept to his son and his daughter. What was his business network worth to him?

Many business owners enter our business organization without having proper health coverage or life insurance. When operating on their own, nobody tells them how important this is. If they gain access to this critical information in their first year of joining a business network, it sets them and their families with this support from that point on. Over the years I have received "Thank You" cards from their widows when they suddenly passed away. They would not have had the insurance if they had not surrounded themselves with successful business owners who were properly insured. What was that worth to their families?

We have had business owners who thought to buy travel insurance to protect themselves because it was recommended in the groups they attended. It can be very costly to get sick in another country without having insurance. A friend of mine outside of the network received a bill for more than $100,000 for a short hospital stay while he was traveling. Many of our members have needed medical help while traveling and I don't recall hearing of anyone who did not have the proper insurance. Why? Because insurance is regularly a topic in networking groups. Not being insured is a costly mistake our members don't usually make because they were educated and warned. What is that worth?

Outside of our network I hear of misfortunes all the time. I knew a lady who hired a general contractor and gave him $70,000 up front; he disappeared with the money. I have met people who hired website designers, gave them $5000 or more and never got a completed website. There are business owners who spend thousands of dollars a year on marketing without any measurable results. These kinds of things do not happen much in a business network where members meet weekly. It would be embarrassing for the owner of the misdeed to show up. Imagine a website designer meeting with a group every week who did not produce the promised website. It would be uncomfortable to attend.

Accountability is why some of the best service in the world is found through the members of professional business networks. Our members have accountability. We have accountability. We want to do an excellent job and we give extra care when we look after referrals given to us through our network. What is the value of that?

When we take all these factors into account, what is it worth to be part of a reputable business network?

Want to become part of a thriving, modern group of networkers?

Fill out the application here at

https://bit.ly/CIBNapplication

CHAPTER FIVE

Getting It Done Better and Faster

As entrepreneurs, we have this "get it done" kind of spirit. We are often pioneers laying the trail and going in a direction where nobody has gone before. We fancy ourselves as disruptors of the status quo. We are like captains of our own ship. When we find ourselves surrounded by people who think like employees, it makes us feel like we are all alone in the world. The result is a natural tendency to depend more upon ourselves than anybody else.

Moving From Diy To Scaling

The problem is that we can't build an Empire or do anything of real significance solely on our own effort. Anything big that would provide a legacy is going to need a team. Business coaches will tell us that to scale we are going to need to surround ourselves with people who are smarter than us. We are going to put these people in charge of the pieces we are not naturally good at and even some of the things we are good at. Eventually, we are going to need to give away everything we do so that our venture can multiply. How do we start thinking like somebody who builds teams and lifts individuals rather than somebody who tries to do everything themselves?

Growing Through Networking

Belonging to a network is more than a business decision. The new and modern networks have a support system for entrepreneurs that draws the people we need to help us succeed. As we meet with people every week and we get to know, like and trust them, they start to feel like that about us. It becomes natural to use the group subcontractor to help us get a job done. As we hang around other people who delegate, it may not be long before we will be using the services of a virtual assistant to help us get our more menial tasks done.

Everything we do starts to become easier as we surround ourselves with people in our network who have better methods of getting it done. When we isolate ourselves in our own office, or our store front business, we have no idea about shortcuts that we could take, hacks that we could use, social media methods that work, or marketing that pays us back. How would we learn to use these things when we are all alone in the world?

Is There Room For Brick-And-Mortar In B2B Networking?

Entrepreneurs often isolate themselves from the world and feel like nobody understands them. As we have developed in-person meetings, or hybrid models we would send sales teams out into the streets. They would go from business to business handing out business cards and inviting people to come to one of the meetings being held nearby. We often had to explain to them what networking was. The message had not yet reached store front businesses that there was help for them. Some of them had heard of the local Chamber of Commerce, and many told us that the Chamber was not a fit for their business. They acknowledged that traditional, old-fashioned networking wasn't meeting their needs and they were not looking for any alternative solutions.

We met large numbers of business owners who had never encountered networking. We had to begin from the beginning explaining what we meant when we used the term. We learned that some thought networking meant they had a LinkedIn account. Some thought networking was referring to the cable they had laid to put in their land-line phones. Others had been to one of our competitor's groups and they felt networking meant a lot of volunteerism and demanding work that would not pay them back for their time. Few had any idea that networking could be profitable.

Did you know that 80% of all business owners do not do any networking? It is also true that 80% of businesses go out of business in their first five years. Yet in our business network where we got started in an oil-and-gas city and during one of the worst oil recessions in history, we went close to a decade without losing a single member to business failure in our groups. How is that possible? I would love to take full credit for that, but it was not me. It was the group looking after the group which was the deciding factor that pointed our members toward success.

"A rising tide raises all ships." ~ Winston Churchhill

A good business network is going to help a person not just get the lead they need but also equip that person for overall success in their business through a variety of methods. The community and its support will help a business owner keep their attitude positive and their business in the black even in tough times.

Through our network, we have access to media in print and media over the airways and all have opportunities to influence how we think about things. I recall reading a report at one time saying the real estate market was dead. We would meet realtors who were out there on their own and they would tell us times were so tough. They said they could not get a sale to save their lives. They accepted what the media was reporting as fact, and it affected how they were performing in their business. We, however, created our own unique economy inside our business network. As our members would meet around the table, the mortgage broker would talk about the deals he had put into place, and the life insurance agent would mention the success he was having.

The bakery owner would bring baked goods and hand them out around the room while he was talking about how business was up 17% this year. The print and promo guy would talk about his 35% increase in sales over the last two years. The florist was selling flowers at every meeting and the bookkeeper was hiring staff to keep up. Many of these results were happening because we were not buying into the status quo. It's also hard to go out of business when somebody keeps slipping a warm lead under your door.

THE KNOW, LIKE, AND TRUST FACTOR

The network members would help each other in other ways, too. The marketing expert in the room would talk about the program he was using and the effect the program was having with his clients. As a rule, it seemed at least one of the members would try him out and experience a positive result. Then they would talk about the outcomes that member had and soon that would encourage other members to try out the marketing program. Each of them would be better off than if they tried to buy their marketing online from somebody they found through Google. When you are working with strangers doing business be it on the internet or next door, it comes with increased risk when the work being done is not accountable to anybody.

One should also question marketers who send us spam-like solicitations through email. If their marketing methods worked so well, why are they not using them themselves? If they have a service that is so great at getting leads from a website, why would they not just build a website of their own and use it to get leads? Why are they sending us emails saying they have a great service? They are clearly not practicing what they preach. Yet, year after year we hear the woes told by business owners who report they spent money on a system that did not work.

We often hear about somebody who paid for a website that never got built. They hired someone they met outside of the business network, paid $5000 up front, and were out the money. That sort of thing seldom happens inside a business network because these people meet every week. It gets really embarrassing if that person hasn't delivered the website. It's a little extra pressure on a website builder to do a decent job and finish the work in a timely fashion. It is just one of the kinds of costly mistakes that can happen to lone rangers out in the wilderness.

In my first year in business, I made an $18,000 mistake. That was more money than I had made the year before as a pastor. The error almost crippled me permanently. Fortunately, I found networking, and I surrounded myself with mentors and coaches, and I got a lot smarter faster. How much money did I save over the years by avoiding mistakes? It is hard to tell but I would estimate its millions of dollars to this date.

THE PRICELESS BUSINESS EDUCATION FACTOR

Our members were learning things from one another like social media tips. Our social media boot camps alone were saving some members thousands of dollars as they would choose to do the work of writing and making posts themselves rather than hire somebody. Others saved themselves headaches and money because they now knew what the person they hired should be doing. They now knew exactly what they wanted to do and even if they did not want to do it themselves, they knew who to hire because there was somebody in the network who would get that job done well for a fair price. They now knew what to tell them to do so there were clear and achieved measurable results from their efforts. How many hours and weeks and years of potentially wasted time might you save by knowing a better path? How do you put a price tag on that?

Over the years we learned things like time-blocking, a system that saved us hours and years of time. We became more efficient as we nailed goalsetting by achieving those goals regularly. We did things like create operations manuals and mission statements and uncovered our core values. These practices saved us money because we were not hiring and rehiring people over and over again and taking up our precious time in retraining. We learned to video record our training for core staff people so we would not have to keep taking time from our schedules to train new ones when the last one quit or was let go.

These were some of the changes to our businesses that made an effective difference, but what about the life hacks? Some were worth millions of dollars. We had mortgage brokers who taught us how to pay for one mortgage and have five houses to retire with instead of just one. We learned how we could be involved in land banking and get returns of three to four times what we invested in less than ten years. We all carried insurance and had less life and death situations that might have destroyed the legacies we had built.

Let us not forget what we learned about health and wellness. This is an industry that is bound and gagged with strict boundaries about what they can say and how they can say it. At one of our networking meetings, a chiropractor told us that motion is lotion for our sore back. Through our members, we learned of products which were available and yielded remarkable results. It's called education and learning through word of mouth. Members tell their network about a solution and the news travels. Our business networks provide a place for this to happen naturally and being involved in a group like this opens opportunities to get answers to life's struggles. Please note that we do not condone, nor do we encourage the breaking of any rules related to the promotion of health care products. We simply offer a space for network marketing to take place.

OWNING A BUSINESS AND HAVING A COACH

Business coaches and mentors helped us get where we wanted to go faster. Without having someone outside of our chaos looking at things, we grow holes in our expenses, and we miss money left on the table where profits could have been. When we are out there with no supporting network, we cannot expect ourselves to know everything. We wonder, "What is a business coach and what could coaching do for me?" We have no idea why we would need them. We also don't have any clue as to how to tell a good business coach from a bad one. We don't know what questions to ask. We have no frame of reference. We sadly will hire an out of work engineer that just finished a weeklong course instead of finding a successful businessowner with a history of making good decisions. A business network weeds out the worst coaches because only a successful business coach can afford to pay membership fees. Great business coaches are also appreciative of networking training, and they see the value of being part of a bigger tribe. A lone sheep should never take advice from a lone wolf.

All in all, this business community was more like a family than it was a network. It was not uncommon for us to become close friends and even be included in our home at Christmas time. As we moved into the online world, many of our online celebrations featured our additional family members, our pets and our grandchildren. The business network was, indeed, affecting every part of our lives in an incredibly positive way and everything in our lives was getting done better and faster.

NETWORKING = WORKING YOUR NETS

Think of networking as working one's nets. Everything works more effectively if we work together. Make a picture in your mind's eye of what a net looks like. Do you know what are the strongest points of a fishing net? The strongest points are at the knots where every piece of rope is joined together. The spaces between the knots are where the ropes are the weakest. If the net is going to break, it will not be at the knot where the net is reinforced. We found that the more we worked together in the network, the stronger we became. It was like we were able to create the knots in the net.

We used the metaphor of the net as we figured out a social media strategy that continues to work to this day. The average entrepreneur has less than 1000 connections online. With so few connections, there would be no point to hiring somebody to make us pretty things for our social media marketing. We would be shouting our message into an empty room. This is the reason most people's social media marketing campaigns do not bring them any fruit. With all the social media experts in the world today, there's only a handful who will tell you that you need more connections for it to be effective. In fact, if you have less than 10,000 connections you may as well not have any at all. That number tends to overwhelm most entrepreneurs, so we made it part of our networking success path to help people figure out how to bring on a few at a time and build these numbers gradually over a few years. The larger the connection numbers, the stronger the online presence. That online component can then be a positive factor with their in-person networking, or the Zoom meetings where they are doing online networking.

Imagine if you were getting warm leads every month through your business network, and you had a social media campaign that was working. Imagine if you learned how to create an automated email sequence and it continued to work for you even while you were sleeping. These things can all be attained through participating in a business network because that is where you find the professionals who can do it for you, or the training so you can do it for yourself. I have encountered business owners who felt they were too busy to take any additional training and for that reason some would not even take the networking training. That is a hugely unfortunate and wasted opportunity because networking is easy, fun, and incredibly productive when done effectively.

If we wanted to learn to play guitar, what would we do first? We would sign up to take an online course. We might start watching YouTube videos we get for free and that would lead to taking an online course we paid for. Then we might decide to hire a teacher or a coach. As we become more proficient and have more practice, it is likely we would find mentors we looked up to. If we wanted to continue to grow in our skill, we would look for opportunities to practice and perform. We may even start song writing. The deeper we would get into guitar playing, the more we might invest in it by buying a more expensive guitar.

When it comes to networking, the steps are similar. It is true that some people are naturally better connectors than others, just like some people can pick up an instrument and start to play a song without training. But to get genuinely good at something, one usually needs to invest sufficient time, effort and training into whatever it is they are trying to accomplish. Why would networking be any different?

I succeeded early in my business career using networking as a tool because I had mentors and coaches who showed me how to do it. These were not the regular business coaches that I later met in the network. I found that most business coaches would tell their clients they needed to go out networking, but they had no idea about where to send them. They also did not give them the simple how-to methods that would work, because they did not know these methods. Business coaching was their area of expertise, not networking. Networking is its own thing. We need a mentor and a coach in networking to master networking. We do not want to find a life insurance agent who runs a networking meeting once a month. We are looking for networking experts who run a professional network for doing business, who have experience in pulling together a group of people and who know how to get business from the process. That is the person who can show us how to get it done.

Over the last few years, I have mentored thousands of people to become more efficient networkers and who have profited from the experience. We have built courses and manuals that have been effective for those who are a "do-it-yourself" kind of person. Most people, however, benefit from a little hand holding. It is not enough for me to tell someone how to do it. It is better if I show you how to do it and if I take you by the hand and help you do it.

The value of networking is massive. The potential revenue increase, the saving of time, and the compiled knowledge gained through the process is mountainous.

Networking is fun. The gains are achievable. All the help we would need is available. So, let's get started.

Here is the QR code to join in for a free online community and find out more about how to network with CIBN Connect. Start posting about your business as soon as you join.

Visit the CIBN Connect event page at https://cibnconnect.com/cibn-events

To see modern networking done right check out the CIBN Connect events

CHAPTER SIX

The Infomercial That Converts

There are several ways one could do an infomercial. The most common way is to stand up and utter whatever pops into our head without any script or thought on how to make our infomercial effective. That will not be one of the methods we focus on. That method is as tired, old, and useless as traditional business networking. Let's look at other more effective methods.

In this chapter we will explore five methods of doing an infomercial. As we go through each one, we will find they get increasingly more effective for getting the desired results. As we deliver the information, we will have a single ask. We will never try to ask for two things in a single infomercial. If we want an appointment booked with us as our outcome, then that is what we will ask for. If we want everyone in the group to subscribe to our YouTube channel, then that is our ask. If we ask for two things at once, the listeners will haul off and do nothing as fast as possible.

One Thing At A Time

From my experience of personally running over 8,000 networking meetings, I highly recommend you have only one ask. The most common reason for not getting referrals through networking is because we have been asking for more than one thing. By the time we have finished describing the second thing, the listeners will have forgotten the first thing and will no longer be interested in giving us what we ask for. Therefore, we ask for only one thing at a time.

If we have two businesses, we need to save one for another meeting. There are only 60 seconds in an infomercial. Half of nothing is still nothing, so do not divide up the time. What do we really want today? We want focus and attention. And we want to have a specific target market where we are centering our attention.

Who Is Your Client? Who Is Your Customer?

Have you done the work on what your ideal client looks like? Do you have a client avatar? Think about the current customers you already have. What things do they have in common? Which ones do you most enjoy doing business with? Who would you like to have more of as clients or customers?

I once had somebody tell me they wanted to do business with people who had small children. When I asked them if they had any children, they said they did not. How can we relate to this clientele if this is not who we ourselves are? We should not pick a group of people because it sounds good, or because it is trendy. Pick a target group based on experience. We may have a desire to serve single mothers but unless we are a single mom, it is going to be difficult to get this group to relate to us. Having pity on a certain group does not equate to empathy. Empathy is where we feel what they feel and that comes easiest through shared experiences.

As a new business owner, we should be careful to pick a target group that can purchase our product or service. We should not pick a group to which to market based on our feelings. If you want to be in business five years from now, your buyers will be important. I once met an entrepreneur who was starting out by selling a $5000 product to teenagers. He is no longer in business. That was a difficult target market to reach. Few teens have that much money to make a purchase. He was driven by the desire to help youth. As a priority when starting a business, I recommend focussing on making the money needed for survival. This is not to say that a portion of the income should not go toward charitable endeavours. As prosperity grows, we can dedicate more money and more time to philanthropic preferences. A business needs to exist to provide income for the business owner and it requires an investment of time to develop and grow the business. Helping others may be a happy happenstance and a secondary reason for doing business, but if we run our business like a non-profit, we may have no profit from which to pay ourselves or support our loved ones. Not-for-profit businesses are cause-driven, and they sound wonderful, but passion will not pay the bills. Successful cause-driven businesses are usually the second, or third businesses of people who have already made millions. They are not often the first business undertaking of the new entrepreneur. Consider these things as we look at potential avatars and target markets on which to focus our attention.

SCRIPTING THE INFOMERCIAL

As we create our infomercial, let's also create a script that we follow. We cannot tell if our infomercial is working if we change it every time we talk. We cannot tell if people are consistently booking appointments with us if we use our script at only one meeting where there are just twenty people in attendance. We must say the same infomercial in front of at least twenty people on dozens of occasions. And the first twenty times are only practice. We get better as we say it and we become more comfortable with each delivery. Therefore, the first few times should not be considered in the overall data related to whether our infomercial landed a sale. It is data that gives us the numbers telling us if something is working. Winging it and changing the words continuously do not contribute to data. Winging it is for wing night. Winging it is not a solid marketing strategy. Creating scripts and sticking to the script is a much better plan.

Make a plan and work the plan. Never stray from the plan.

#1 The Basic Infomercial

The basic infomercial is the most common in a business network. It is the one we will hear given by most people most of the time because they have never spent time working on exactly what they should say, and this matter-of-fact delivery is what comes easiest. The only advantage of doing a basic information infomercial is that it will give us practice and start to help us feel comfortable in front of a group of people. So, if it gets us going, it is certainly better than nothing. However, one does not want to stay here forever.

The basic infomercial is where we simply state our name, and the name of our company and we describe what we do and ask for a lead.

At an online meeting it would sound something like this: "Hello everyone. My name is Christine Block, and I am a bookkeeper. If you are currently trying to do the books for your business by yourself, you might want to hire me or refer me to your friend who is behind in their bookkeeping. My company is called XYZ Bookkeeping, and I will put my Information into the chat. Please book an appointment with me."

This type of infomercial is easy. If we get stuck because we are nervous talking in front of a group of people, these are the words that will come to us most naturally. Use this infomercial until you have the confidence to try something else.

Those who are listening are not likely to feel any emotion in response to this infomercial and may not even remember it. **The basic infomercial can get lost in the "sea of sameness" as everyone repeats similar information one at a time at a networking meeting. So how will you ever stand out?**

#2 The Testimony Infomercial

An effective way of getting people to think of somebody to refer to us is to tell them a story to which they can relate. Specifics help people think about who they can recommend to us. This is where it is helpful to know our target market or our avatar because we can then describe that person and help the listener feel the connection to our story.

When we are doing a testimony infomercial, we will have to give up our attachment to the regular kind of infomercial. It stands on its own and it is not something we add on at the end because we won't have enough time.

Whenever we are asked to speak at an event, whether it is for one minute, twenty minutes or for hours, more than anything else we need to respect the timekeeper. People may be polite if we go overtime but that does not mean they like it. They may smile on the outside but on the inside, they may become infuriated. Everybody else stuck to the time, and we need to stick to the time boundaries as well. It is disrespectful to everybody else in the event to continue speaking after our allotted time.

The best way to prepare for a testimony infomercial is to make notes so we can stick to the story. At the beginning of our sixty seconds, we are not going to say our name and we are not going to talk about our company. If there is time, we may be able to tack those items on at the end. If there is not time, it is not a problem. If we have done this correctly, our testimony will interest people in the room; they will ask for a connection or they will book an appointment on the spot when we share our calendar link in the chat.

Think about the testimonies that customers have shared with you about your work. **Who has said something about you that would make a relevant story with a great outcome?** Matching your ask to your story would be ideal. Let's hear from our bookkeeper, Christine, again.

"Last week one of my clients sent me an email that said, "Thank you, Christine, for all your hard work and effort with my bookkeeping over the last year. It has given me a great deal of peace knowing that my books are looked after. Before you came along, I had all my receipts in a box, and my bookkeeping was a mess. I was afraid of tax audits, and I could barely sleep. You have taken a great burden off me, and I thank you again." My name is Christine Block, and I like to help you get your receipts out of the box and into Quick Books, so you can relax and spend your time doing the things that need to be done in your business. Who do you know that should book an appointment with me?"

In an online meeting, Christine would want to put her name and contact information in the chat with a calendar link to book time with her immediately. As a reminder, she might include her ask with her link. Later in the meeting, she will want to post ALL of her contact information, such as phone number, email address, LinkedIn URL and calendar link. But right now at the end of speaking, she should only share her calendar link to keep focus on the one thing that she is asking for. One thing, one ask. This is what works the best.

In a testimony infomercial, you share a quick story that a client told about you. In some cases, we may be able to share who the client was, but oftentimes we will not be able to say their name because of client confidentiality. In that case, we should just say, "I had a client who said this," or possibly "I have a client who is a realtor who said this." No matter what industry we represent, we will need to use our discretion about using the real names of clients.

A testimony infomercial is more powerful than simply stating who we are and what we do. It allows our listeners to hear a testimony and someone's story is always more interesting than straight facts. **Those who are listening to testimony infomercials often report that the story helps them think of someone who could be interested in the services of the speaker.**

#3 A Results-Based Infomercial

A results-based infomercial is where we are telling the story of the results we achieved with a client. It differs from the testimony informational where we are telling the story somebody has said about us. A testimony infomercial may say good things about our work but may not share the exact results.

When we report the results achieved working with a client instead of asking for something from everybody in the room, it gives evidence we know what we are doing. It attracts people to want to do business with us as a desired expert. It also feels incredibly good to report the success story where we had an impact in someone's business or someone's life. Once again, we would not necessarily divulge the name of the client to protect their confidentiality.

And, once again, in the interests of respecting time, we cannot begin this infomercial with our name and details about our services. To be on point with the time, we only want to share the story.

Here is an example of a results-based testimonial using our bookkeeper.

"About two months ago, one of my clients was contacted by the government and she was genuinely concerned. She was about to go through an audit. Because I had been regularly doing her books and I had dealt with the government before, I contacted the department on her behalf. The good news is I was able to bring a quick resolution to their questions. She was able to avoid an audit and all the stress which comes with that. Do you know somebody who is concerned about getting audited? I would like to help them. My name is Christine, and this is my calendar link to book an appointment."

The main difference between the testimony infomercial and the results-based infomercial is how the networker tells the story. The testimony infomercial has us repeating the words of our client as close as possible to how they said it. The results-based Infomercial does not require us to quote the client exactly. We are sharing the problem the client had and affirming the problem was solved. We do not need to discuss how it was solved because that will not fit into our sixty-second window of time. After we share that we solved the problem, the natural course of action would be to ask, "Who do you know that has this problem?" This is a specific question that triggers a memory in our listeners. It is a highly effective infomercial, and it has the added benefit of us feeling good as we say it.

Those who are listening to results-based infomercials often report they understand what the speaker is saying with ease, and they are immediately impressed with their expertise.

#4 The Personality Infomercial

The personality infomercial is more difficult than the others because it requires a basic understanding of the personality types. Over the years there have been a number of prominent sorting mechanisms developed where personality styles are organised into four basic categories. Popular methods include Colors, DISC Assessment, Animals, and Sea Creatures. Myers Briggs, another device, split four major groupings into sixteen categories. These sorting mechanisms often tend to find you scoring higher on at least one category.

To keep this as simple as possible, we are going to name each of these four personality styles according to an older model which you may have seen before. Would you believe this model was first introduced by Hippocrates in ancient Greece?

 No matter which system you prefer, understanding personality types offers incredibly useful information for giving an infomercial to a large group of people as well as for making sales to individuals. When we understand what is important to someone, we can hit their hot buttons and answer the questions that matter to them very quickly. **Learning about personality differences is helpful in our personal life as well as our business relationships. It is easier to build lasting relationships with people if we understand them better.**

When we employ this method as we are addressing a group, we can safely assume that everyone in the room is falling somewhere into these four categories. There is going to be a mixture. It would be ideal if we could give those in attendance a test and gather the results beforehand because then we would know "who is who in the zoo," so to speak. That is not likely to happen. The good news is we do not need to know everyone's test score. We can simply operate from the assumption there are going to be some from every category present.

People tend to score high in one these personality types. The characteristics of that personally type come across as prominent components of who they are, and we would call this their primary personality type. Then there will be the next personality type that would score higher than the third and fourth category but not as high as the first. This would be the secondary personally type.

As I have already stated, we could use this approach to do an infomercial or an introduction. It involves being mindful of the words you choose. When you do this well, your audience will feel your commitment. In some cases, it could literally raise the hair on the backs of their necks. Everyone in the room will think we are speaking directly to them! This is a hugely powerful way to connect with our audience and to do an infomercial that makes an impact.

As we learn about each personality type, we are also going to discover the one key question that needs to be answered for each of them so they can be satisfied we are somebody with whom they want to meet. A well-done personality style infomercial will deeply touch every person in the room. Let's have a look at the personality types.

The Sanguine Personality

The Sanguine Personality is an outgoing personality who likes to talk with their hands and make big motions. Often, they stand out in a group not only by their boisterous and fun-loving behavior but also by the bright colors they wear, the big earrings, the big hair, and bright socks and ties. They especially like having a fun time and are often the life of the party. In fact, having fun is their one concern. The Sanguine Personality wants to know if we are fun people. They want to know if the thing we are offering is any fun. **They have no patience to wait for our answer, and if we do not answer this, they won't want to meet with us because they don't like to do things that are boring. This is their number one complaint about people and things in life. They can't stand boring.**

The Choleric Personality

The Choleric Personality is the second most impatient person at the party. When I say he is second, he is right behind the Sanguine Personality by a hair. There is not much margin here. In working with Choleric Personalities, we may think they are ahead of the Sanguines in lacking patience because they are the ones who will tell us to be quiet when we talk too much. However, the Sanguine Personality already told us to shut up in their mind. They did not say it aloud because they would not ruin their party. Just know it happened in seconds as soon as we started to talk about anything that was not fun for them. **The Choleric Personality will usually tell us to stop talking about five minutes after we enter their office, but they were actually thinking it three minutes into the conversation. Have you ever had someone interrupt**

you in the middle of a conversation where it was your turn to talk? This could be the announcement that you have been tuned out. It's time to move on.

This behavior is typical of the hard driving workaholic that is the Choleric Personality. **Along with being a staunch extrovert, he spares no time for beating about the bushes. He likes to get things done.** Have you ever gone into somebody's office to make a presentation and they told you to stop talking and just tell them what the bottom line was? This is a Choleric Personality. They don't like to wait around, and they make decisions quickly. They don't want us to author a book when we enter their office. **They want us to give them the reasons why they should do what we want them to do in three sentences or less. Then they want you to shut up so they can make a decision. If we keep talking, we are going to talk them out of deciding in our favor.** The key question they want us to answer is, "What are the fast facts?" They may also want to know if we can get it done. They like to hear words like efficiency, and profitability. These words should come at the beginning of the presentation and not sixteen pages into it.

This is somebody who will tell us they gave us five minutes and now they are upset because it is five minutes they are not going to get back. Many entrepreneurs have this as a primary or a secondary personality style, so to be in alignment with their priority we should say things like "I get things done," in our messaging or we will lose them.

If we are handing this person a report, we should put the fast facts on the first page. They really like a good summary. If we hand them a hundred pages, it is going into the garbage the second we leave. For the best results, we want to give them quick CLIFFS NOTES.

The Analytical or Melancholy Personality Style

The analytical person wants to know all the details.

Have you ever seen a website that is seven pages deep with information? **The Sanguine Personality is only looking for the bright flashing picture at the top of the page, and the Choleric Personality is looking for the summary right under that bright picture at the top of the page. However, the Analytical Personality is going to read all seven pages.** Twice. They want to know everything there is to know before they decide.

When we are doing a sixty-second infomercial, we cannot give this person all the details. However, we can tell them in our infomercial that we have all the details. It may be enough to pique their interest. They also love to hear we are well organized and that we have a plan. Structure and scheduling are particularly important to this personality style.

The Phlegmatic Personality Style

The Phlegmatic Personality is the toughest personality style to figure out. The Phlegmatic Personality is easy going and they blend in with the people who are around them. **They are like chameleons, and they try to fit in. However, if we get to know them, we will see they are the kind of people who like to work hard during the day and rest after eight hours.** The Phlegmatic is a guy who comes home from work and likes to have supper, lay on the couch, and watch the hockey game. He feels like he has put in a good day's work and it's time to relax.

Phlegmatic people have one burning concern, and they are quite easy to satisfy if we know what that is. **All they want to know is if this is good for their family.** If they do not have a family, they might ask the question another way such as, "How is your product or service going to impact your family?" It's all about the family.

I have a phlegmatic friend who is single. She has never been married and she doesn't have any kids. Still, she is easy to identify because when we visit her home, or if we go into her office, there are pictures of her extended family everywhere. She has pictures of her nieces and her nephews, and she likes to attend every family event; she talks fondly about her family at every opportunity. If we are visiting somebody's office and we see a lot of pictures of their family, the chances are they are primarily phlegmatic unless, of course, their wife decorated their office and she's the phlegmatic one. We do learn to manage our lives based on those around us, but when we make our own choices, we usually lean in hard to the personality style that is most comfortable for us.

Analytical people tend to dress in gray and beige, but they may wear a bolder tie if their sanguine wife gave it to them as a gift. Color choices will not tell us everything, but when we see a pattern emerging, it is sending us an important message not to be ignored.

Let's go back to Christine and see how she does the Personality Style Infomercial:

"Do you find bookkeeping boring? I love numbers and I am a fun bookkeeper who will make your record keeping process easy and stress free. I am like superwoman with a calculator! I swoop in and get things done and look after the details so you can spend your time focusing on your business. Let me help you create more profit so you can give your family the time they deserve from you. If you want to be highly effective and organized in your bookkeeping without having to do all the work yourself, then I am your bookkeeper! I am Christine Block, and I am the solution you are looking for. This is my calendar link."

Examine the Personality Chart and think about how these key questions are relevant to your industry. **What could you say in your infomercial that would show you are fun to be with, that family is important to you, that you have all the details, and that you get things done.** It is not easy to pull these details out of our hat. This is an infomercial you will want to practice. It is important to write this one out and rehearse it to make sure it fits within the time constraints of sixty seconds. As we say these words, the information and the excitement should build like a crescendo, so people feel the passion in what we are saying. When this information is delivered properly, it should evoke an emotional response. People might experience chills going down their spine as they connect to our words.

Sanguine

Strengths	Weaknesses
Sociable	Impulsive
Outgoing	Chronically late
Charismatic	Forgetful
Oozes confidence	Shameless
Lively	Talks too much
Pleasant	Talks too loud
Optimistic	Too happy
Warm-hearted	Easily distracted
Spontaneous	Not a good follower
Prevents dull moments	Easily bored
Apologizes quickly	Self-absorbed
Makes friends easily	Over exaggerates
Loves fun	Appears unauthentic

Is this any fun?

Choleric

Strengths	Weaknesses
Ambitious	Aggressive
A natural leader	Inflexible
Focused	Domineering
Practical	Rude and tactless
Makes plans	Impatient
Solves problems	Argumentative
Assesses things quickly	Doesn't like to relax
Confident	Doesn't like emotion
Motivating	Workaholic
A delegator	Low on empathy
Makes decisions fast	Too busy for others
Usually right	Intolerant
Great in an emergency	Demands loyalty

What is the bottom line?

Phlegmatic

Strengths	Weaknesses
Relaxed	Shy
Quiet and calm	Fearful of change
Kind	Stubborn
Consistent	Can be lazy
Steady and faithful	Passive-aggressive
Affectionate	Indecisive
Accepting	Unenthusiastic
Peacemaking	Not goal oriented
Diplomatic	Overly compromising
Rational	Undisciplined
Curious	Sarcastic
Observant	Discouraging
Easily makes friends	Non-participative

Is this good for my family?

Melancholic

Strengths	Weaknesses
Thoughtful	Perfectionist
Cautious	Overly cautious
Considerate	Can't make a decision
Very organized	Procrastinator
Loves to plan	Prone to depression
Detailed	Pessimistic
Schedule orientated	Moody and melancholic
Highly creative	Anal retentive
Musical and poetic	Difficult to please
Inventive	Tunnel vision
Independent	Discontent
Prevents problems	Plays the martyr
Loves processes	Discouraged by failure

Can you give me details?

#5 The Hybrid Infomercial

We have learned a lot about how to do an infomercial that generates impact with as many people in the audience as possible. Once we understand each of these infomercials, we can use this knowledge to put together a hybrid.

We know what is important to people, and we know the kinds of problems we solve. The hybrid infomercial hits the hot buttons of most personalities by asking provocative questions. Once again, we do not start out by saying our name and listing our services. That information may be added in the middle or at the end. **What we want to start with is two or three intense provocative questions that knocks the listeners a little bit off track. Everybody else in the room started their infomercial by saying their names and then they listed all the things that they do. The crowd is bored stiff, so we will begin by waking them up with a strong provocative question designed to make them think.** Let's see how Christine our bookkeeper will manage this:

"Do you know somebody who keeps all their receipts in a box and then lose sleep for three weeks at tax time because they do not have everything together? Have you ever met anyone who didn't know how to read their balance statement and they don't understand what their income and expenses are each month? Do you know anyone who is going through an audit or is afraid of getting audited? I help busy business owners get their bookkeeping done on time, so they have peace of mind. This frees them up to be the creative, and fun, family loving people they were meant to be. My name is Christine, and this is my link to book an appointment with me."

In Conclusion:

Which one of these informercials speaks to you? Where would you like to start? Read them over again and choose your favorite. Then take out at pen and write a script following the method closely. Practice the script to be sure that it can be delivered in less than 60 seconds.

To create an infomercial that converts, one needs to create a script that works.

We need to use the script over and over so we can keep track of the results. Scripts should also be created for the one-on-one, the sales presentation, presenting the proposal, and for the follow-up. Without a script we do not have a sales process that can be improved. If we are networking without having a sales process, we will fail in business. Leads are of no value if we suck at selling.

To create scripts that work and to practice them, and to develop a winning sales strategy, you will want to join the SALES PRO program on this page. We turn introverts and grandmothers into sales superstars with this program!

https://www.cibn.club/join-sales-pro-page

CHAPTER SEVEN

IT'S MEETING TIME

Now that we have written the script for our testimonial, we are ready to go out and start networking! Where should we go?

There are so many kinds of networking events we could attend. There are live and in-person meetings where we could have lunch and meet other people. There are mixers where they sometimes have beer and wings. There are dedicated events like conferences and training events. Where should we spend our networking time?

If we are taking our networking seriously, we are looking for measurable outcomes. That should mean we want to go networking in places where we can, indeed, network. The event should not focus on something else with a little networking on the side. If there is a speaker talking for an hour, this is not a networking event. This is a speaker's event, and it will not have the same outcomes.

There are two main categories of events, although there could be many subcategories. Let's talk about in-person events and online events. Any other events would fall under these primary category headings. The first events we will examine are the in-person events.

IN-PERSON NETWORKING MIXERS

In-person events are fun, and social, and they can be productive, if we are a well-trained, professional

networker. They may not be as efficient as online meetings because of the time it takes to drive there, and the inability to get around to everybody in the room who we want to talk to. Geography is a concern. We can only go to in-person events that are geographically close to us, or at least within our budget to get to them. There are in-person networking events in every city, so which ones should we take advantage of?

We need to establish what professional networking meetings look like, so that we do not end up saying, "I spent a lot of my time and money going to networking meetings and it yielded a low return on my investment." I have been to networking meetings where there was a lot of real networking going on and suddenly the organizers brought out karaoke, or dancing. The music in the place got louder and louder and what happened next was that all the serious networkers went home. Most people who came to this event did not come with their spouse or their significant other, and as soon as that music started, they were instantly reminded they had left their other half at home; they pay their drink bill, and they leave. People who are serious about networking usually avoid musical theater unless they are going out for a musical theater event, and they are attending with their spouse.

As I have already stated, we should look for meetings that focus on networking. An event that has a speaker is not genuinely a networking event. It means we are going to listen to a speaker. If the event is advertised as a networking event and there is a speaker, we should determine if we are likely to find our potential clients and buyers there. Examine the agenda and note the amount of time allotted for networking. **A real networking event provides a suitable amount of time for you to network with other people. It is where they get to talk about what they do, and you get to talk about what you do.** Getting around to speak with as many people as possible and exchanging business cards with them would be highly encouraged. If you get to an event and these things are not happening, the meeting may still have value. Why not think of every event you attend as an opportunity to gain experience and an opportunity to network.

You do not need to ask permission or wait for approval. Always be networking.

When we are attending in-person events, it is a wonderful opportunity to use our scripted infomercial. This will work better if we practice. Many people feel uncomfortable when they are talking to strangers, and introverts often experience feelings of anxiety. There is no magic pill to take away these pains. The best course of action is to practice before we get there. Rehearsing our infomercial in front of the mirror can help and practicing it out loud gives us more confidence to do it in person. When we arrive, this is no time to park yourself on a chair. The more we move around the room to talk to people, the more we will feel our comfort level rise. If we go to an event where we talk to 20 people in an hour, by the end of our first hour we are going to feel more polished. When we do this activity a few times a month, we should expect to feel much more comfortable.

PREPARING FOR FOLLOWING UP

It is a great idea to create a follow-up plan before we attend an in-person networking event. Are we going to try to phone all these people the next day? That is one traditional and outdated method that is highly ineffective. It's not 1959 so let's make a more modern plan. It is better to look in our calendar before we leave for our event and find a two-day spread when we can block some time. If we are wanting to meet people in person, we should pick a location where we can do one meeting after another. Be prepared to book the meetings on the spot while we are at the event. Our one-on-one meeting location may be near the networking event, because we know these people got there that night, so the chances are good they would come back to the area for a one-on-one in the next few days. By using one location for all the meetings I am saving hours of time in driving because they are coming to me. If they do not show up for the meeting, I have my laptop with me and I will be working while I am waiting.

I have an office downtown in my city and this is the location I would use. It is convenient and I already pay for the space. However, when I had no office, I used coffee houses to hold meetings. I always made sure I left a substantial tip for my server as I was using their space for several hours. I wanted them to remember me the next time I came in and I wanted preferential treatment. It would impress people who were meeting me when the server knew my name and knew what my favorite beverages were. My business sometimes takes me to other sectors of my city and to other cities. If possible, I pick a privately-owned establishment where I can get to know the owner and the staff, and I continue to frequent that location rather than jumping around to unfamiliar places.

If I am going out networking on a Monday evening and I know that Thursday and Friday I am going to be in a coffee shop on the west side of the city, I will take a stack of my business cards and I will be sure to carry sticky notes. Business cards often have a glossy finish on them, making it impossible to put our notes directly onto the card itself. As a professional networker, I plot solutions to potential difficulties before I attend the networking event.

As I move through the room talking to each person, I identify my potential prospect by asking mindful questions. When I find the someone who qualifies, I will want to book a one-on-one right there on the spot. I will ask the first prospect if they are available on Thursday morning at 9 o'clock and if they could meet me for coffee at my chosen location. When they agree I will write that information on the sticky note, and I will stick it on the card they gave me. I then place their card at the bottom of my pile. I move to the next prospect, and I ask them if they would like to meet me at 10 o'clock at the same location. If they say "Yes," I repeat the pattern. If they say "No, I could meet you at 1 o'clock in the afternoon" I write that on a sticky note and I put it on the top of my pile. I move on to the next person and I ask them if they would like the 10 o'clock spot. As I do this, I fill each blank spot in succession. I tell each person I will follow up with the directions to our meeting place in an email which I will send this evening or the following morning if this is a late-night event.

As I am working through a networking meeting, I want to make sure that my hands are free, and my pockets have space in them for my growing stack of collected business cards. If I'm going to transfer these to my purse or to a briefcase, I want to make sure that I have some plastic baggies to put them in, or some elastics to keep them together. When we send our confirmations out by email, we want to be sure we are referring to the correct networking event in our messaging. This becomes especially important if we are attending multiple events.

Preparedness wins the game every time. When we have a solid understanding of our calendar, we can immediately book appointments on the spot. It is important as well to have only one ask. I'm not trying to get them to follow me on social media; I am asking them for an appointment. It is one or the other, and it is never both. By having more than one ask, I would be making certain I have no appointments booked. Two asks will amount to nothing more than a nice evening filled with many conversations, warm fuzzy feelings, and no connections for taking next steps with prospects.

Using this method, I once booked 34 meetings from one meeting and had 27 of them show up over three days using the same location. Four sales of $700 each were made immediately that week during those one-on-one sales appointments. Having them come to my office allowed us to meet in a space that offered no distractions. I could give my visitor my undivided attention. As follow-ups were done over the next few weeks, I closed a total of 21 sales. This was an effective use of my networking time, and many business relationships were created that are still intact to this day.

When I am going out networking at local in-person events, I also make sure I have time in my calendar to verify the appointments later that evening or first thing in the morning. I used to do this myself. As I became more successful, I hired an admin assistant who was ready to take that information and deal with it immediately the following morning. **There is no point going out networking if there is no time for the follow-up, or if there is no time to make sure you can confirm the appointments you booked. We should say "No" to attending a networking meeting if we do not have time for these important next steps. We do not want to waste the leads by not giving them the time and attention that they deserve.**

I should also clarify that I was able to achieve these results because I was selling networking packages and everyone in the room at this event was a small business owner. I had something they all wanted. If I were selling something only one third of the room qualified for, the results would have been less impressive. I had three things going for me that most people do not have. First, I am a professional networker who has facilitated more than 8000 networking events and I have participated in countless more. Second, my ideal prospects were in the room, and third, I am a trained and practiced salesperson with a strong process that works.

Most people do not have these results in a room that holds a lot of people. They do not know how to talk to twenty people an hour. They have no processes for sales or follow-ups. They get wowed by the shiny large group of people and they mistake a crowd for a large opportunity. It is a delightful opportunity for a networking professional who knows how to touch base quickly and strategically, gather information and establish leads. It is okay if you do not yet have the skill set to drum up 20 meetings in an hour in any room. Making even a couple of connections could be helpful. The novice networker may get more leads at a weekly B2B event, but larger events should not be ruled out and they are a good place to test one's skills.

WEEKLY IN-PERSON NETWORKING EVENTS

Networking at a weekly event is usually more profitable than networking at a large event. When we go to a large event, assuming this is a new group. we must make a rapid impact with as many as possible and we need to have an excellent process in place for follow-up. Without follow-up, this is a total waste of time. Follow up after large events is often more challenging, and it takes a more professional planned out approach. The attendees at the large event do not know us so anything we get from a large meeting will come from our own efforts in the follow-up process.

When we attend a weekly event, and we are meeting with the same people week after week, it takes away the pressure for creating an instant relationship. We are getting to know, like and trust the people at the event just as they are getting to know, like and trust us. We are building relationships over time. The people in this group will often give us more grace to grow as a business owner. They will give us their preferred business often just because we are in their tribe. It may take a while for them to learn about our business, but they will try harder over the long-term because they see our investment of time and money alongside them within the club.

Over the period of one year, your commitment to a networking group can be most profitable because as people get to know us and feel they can trust us, they will be more inclined to refer business to us. And it could be just exactly that one lead which will turn out to be the needle in the haystack you were hoping to find. A warmed-up referral could have a 50% to 75% closing ratio if approached correctly. You only get pre-qualified, warm leads from relationships that have been built over time and so a weekly networking event is an appropriate place to build relationships that can lead to these higher quality leads.

Many organizations offer weekly in-person meetings to their paying members but there may be some rules involved. One rule might be that there is only one person per industry. If this is the only networking we have available to us, it's better than nothing, but it is not a premium experience. This is traditional and old-fashioned networking; it is fear based and removes competition. Everyone is vying for the spot that is popular. So, what happens when the accountant or the mortgage broker leaves the group? The culture of the group and the priorities of its individual members are challenged as to where their loyalties lie. It may take a while for the new person who fills that seat to attract business their way. A group that is collaborative instead of competitive is in a better position to avoid these issues. There are advantages in collaborative groups because real relationships can be built. If the leadership is effective and the people are of a giving nature, it can work out profitably for you.

The in-person weekly event is where we will get to practice our infomercial and get feedback from the group on how well we delivered it. Opinions are not nearly as important as booked appointments and sales, but when we are starting out, feedback is helpful. Remember that a serious, novice networker is going to seek help to improve their ask, but a professional networker is going to use a scripted infomercial that works, and they are going to run the numbers on how many appointments were booked, and how many sales came from those appointments.

Regular attendance is especially important in these kinds of groups because consistency is the ticket that wins the game. Nobody gets to know, like and trust somebody who is inconsistent in attendance. The group members will also judge us according to our attendance whether they say they do or not. Continually missing meetings, or coming late to meetings, or talking too long in the meetings and not respecting the timekeeper will make us stand out as somebody who is not desirable to do business with.

If we are not getting business from a group of this kind within three months of joining, it is a good idea to pull one of the long-term, successful members aside and ask for their mentorship. Ask them if they would tell us honestly what they think of our infomercial. Ask them why they have not done business with us yet, or why they have not yet given us a referral. Ask them to tell us sincerely if we have any mannerisms that are standing out to them as distracting or unprofessional, and then listen carefully to their answers. Chances are we will not want to hear their answers, but if others are getting business in the group and we are not, then it may not be a problem with the group; it may be us. Be willing to look in the mirror and do some soul searching.

If they come back with criticisms we do not like, the thing to do is ask, "Is this true?" Seek out another seasoned member of the group and ask the same questions. Are they saying similar things? Seize this as an opportunity for self-growth as you face your challenges square on. If we run away crying and declaring, "It is not true. These people are so mean," we will continue to have few clients and few referrals. Be brave and face the information they provided. Look for ways to overcome the stumbling blocks.

I remember one of our team members who did this. When he went in search of answers, he was informed by a trusted mentor that he looked unhappy. The mentor wanted to know if he was content because he looked like he was miserable. The member replied that he was happy and had no idea his face was sending a negative message. He began to watch his reflection when he spoke and realised this was true. He discovered he had what is called a "resting bitch face." (His words, not mine.) This was great news! Now he knew why people were not relating to him quickly. He began practicing smiling in his car for a few minutes before going into a meeting. Upon arriving at an event, he would visit the washroom and stretch his mouth into an upward position. What he did resulted in an immediate improvement in how people were responding to him.

I once asked a mentor these questions and was told something I did not like at all. They said I giggled when I spoke, and that people were not taking me seriously as a result. I found their comments hurtful, and I felt they were untrue, so I sought a second opinion. The second person confirmed it. I discovered that the common denominator in my failures was me. I was the problem. I began to pay attention to this character flaw. I realized that I sometimes giggled because I was nervous and at other times I giggled out of habit. This happened less once I became aware of it. I also discovered that I thought I was genuinely funny. I laughed at my own jokes. I cracked myself up. Once I was aware of how this was happening and when it was happening, I was better able to control the urge to giggle when I talked. Sometimes I still giggle intentionally because it is well timed, or it is a situation where a giggle will be well received. At other times I make a choice to not giggle. When I am discussing serious topics or if I want people to listen carefully, or if I do not want to cause offense, I can make a choice because I am aware now that I have a propensity to giggle.

These weekly in-person groups are an excellent place to work on polishing how we present ourselves and to develop good business acumen. If we are open to learning from successful businesspeople, we can create opportunities for self-improvement at these events.

Another advantage of these groups is they will commonly invite us to do a presentation a few times a year. We will get to talk for ten minutes or more to this group and give more details about what we do. The value of this experience is immeasurable.

MAKING A PRESENTATION TO A GROUP

Have you ever gotten a sales appointment where you were asked to present to a board of directors? How did it go?

For many business owners, presenting sucks. Historically, when they finally got the opportunity to be in front of exactly the right group and given exactly the right opportunity to make the big offer, it was a complete wash out. Why?

They had zero experience speaking in front of groups. Practice is the difference between an amateur and a pro every time. These in-person weekly groups are critical for practicing. Big companies spend millions on focus groups. Here is our low-cost focus group giving us the space to learn. By being a member in a group like this, we will refine our speech and sharpen our presentations. We will become confident and prepare exactly the right presentation that wins. That way, at long last, when we get the "big fish" on the line, we will be ready with the net that works to haul them into the boat.

I know I have already said this, but it is worth repeating. It is important at every networking meeting that we only have one ask. Whenever we stand in front of a group of this nature, it is critical that we ask for one thing and one thing only. If we make our ask an easy thing to do, and we make it plain for them to do it, we increase the possibility for success.

We once had a man who sold jewelry attend a weekly networking meeting we were putting on. After 18 months, he let me know that nobody had purchased any of his jewelry. I helped him to rescript his infomercial and then I suggested that he bring a piece of jewelry each week. He was to bring just one piece of jewelry and not a selection. This was a group of about 25 people in the room so he would bring one piece of jewelry and as he would do his infomercial, he would talk about the kinds of jewelry they had. He would open the box and show the jewelry to the people sitting around him. Then he would pass it around the table. After he was done talking and the price was clearly marked on the box, he began selling a piece of jewelry every week and often he would take three more orders from the others who wanted that piece for their wife as a gift. When Valentine's Day and Mother's Day arrived, he received several orders at once, by showing one piece of jewelry.

Some years ago, we had a man who was in the print and promo business. He would come into a presentation and lay several items out on the table. He would pass around things like pens, and mugs, and notebooks. When he used this method, he tended to get zero sales. When he brought only one package of pens and passed them around with a price sheet for that kind of pen with a sign-up form, he would get several sales. One "ask" always works best.

The same individual began changing his larger presentation using the same approach. Instead of featuring several kinds of items, he would feature only mugs. He would bring three kinds of mugs and talk about the quality of each one and what the price points were. He passed an order sheet to each person as he was talking and encouraged them to make notes on the sheet as he did his presentation. After the first time he made the pivot in his presentation, he made three sales on the spot and two others booked appointments with him to look at other promotional products that week. Other sales for mugs followed over the next few months as people returned to the meetings with their order forms already filled out. One "ask" won the day.

A life insurance agent was getting no traction at the networking meetings. We examined his infomercial and discovered he was asking for too many things and that he was talking about multiple services at the same time. We helped him change his infomercial to be a simple ask and we worked on his ten-minute presentation to focus on referrals only. Using this process, he had his best year ever in the financial services industry.

As his presentation began, he handed out chocolates. Chocolates give people a feeling of nostalgia, and they get all our senses working. We can smell the chocolate, we can taste the chocolate and we can see the chocolate. By engaging three of our five senses, a higher level of participation can be expected from our listeners. He then told stories of the people he had helped in the past (without using their real names of course.) He talked about the results he was able to help his clients achieve. He did not mention the rule of 72 and he left out all the pie graphs and charts. Instead, he just talked about real people with real concerns, and he shared how he gave them peace of mind and solved problems for them.

Our life insurance agent had spent some time thinking about exactly what kind of a client he wanted to have. He looked at some of his best clients, and some of the people who gave him the warmest feeling of reward as he worked with them. He decided that he wanted to meet professional couples such as teachers or engineers in their twenties or thirties who had two or more children. He was looking for people who were having a tough time financially and who probably had more month than money. As he gave a remarkably simple and direct description of what he was looking for, this helped everybody in the room to determine exactly who they knew that fit the description. By being specific with his exact target market, it helped to prompt people to think of a particular person. He passed everybody a sheet of paper asking them to put their name at the top. Then he asked them who they knew as he gave his description.

He asked them who they knew who had recently changed jobs and who they knew who had recently had a baby. He asked them about the young adults in their lives who had bought their first starter home in the last five years. He asked who they knew who had two kids in grade school and who they knew who drove a mini van.

More chocolates were handed out and then he asked each one of these attendees to put phone numbers and email addresses onto the sheets paper with the names of the people they had thought of.

In this way, he was able to collect 13 Sheets at the end of the meeting. I watched as he gathered papers with the contact information of five or more people written beside each name.

Again, preparedness wins the game.

In-Person Meeting Tips

- Have something to hand out besides a business card or a piece of paper so you are remembered tomorrow.

- Create a follow up plan before the event.

- Have a small plastic bag that zips shut or a container to store the business cards you collect. Label it with the date and the event.

- Take sticky notes and a good pen.

- Have a solid understanding of your calendar so you can immediately book appointments on the spot.

- Have only one ask: to set an appointment.

- Book one-on-one meetings on the spot.

Online Networking Meetings

There are presently many kinds of networking meetings we can attend online. As previously mentioned, I personally would avoid anything that was free. Free events often tend to attract people who don't want to spend money. Being in business is about attracting people who are willing to spend money, isn't it?

Online, we want to look for networking meetings where the chats are open. If we are attending a Zoom meeting where the person running the meeting has closed all the chats, then it is going to be difficult to make an appointment with somebody who is in the meeting. **We should avoid meetings where people are not encouraged to put their contact information into the** chat area.

Networking is for networking. It is not for coming to listen to a speaker or taking a course. Avoid pep rallies, social activities, and time wasters unless that is what you want. Do not call these events networking meetings and do not track the time spent there as time spent networking. It is not. It is something different.

Practice your infomercial so it is on point and perfectly timed. Always pay attention to the timer in the meeting, and if we do not see one, be sure to time yourself by using your phone, watch, or computer.

In an online meeting we can have our information ready to post into the chat saved somewhere on our computer in a document where we can now just copy and paste it. As for timing, it is best to paste it at the end of what we say. If it is a lively meeting and the chat is moving along quickly, our post may be lost. We can post it again once or twice. Do not post it twenty times because that is rude and excessive. However, most professional networkers will post it two or three times because they know it will get lost in the feed, or that people may be coming into the meeting late. And if they come into the meeting late, they will not be able to see the posts that were made prior to them arriving.

We should be willing to post all our relevant contact information. Networking is not for the secret service. It's not a good place to be if we are in the witness protection program. People will want to get to know us, like us, and trust us and they cannot do that if they cannot find our contact information. We should also note that the information we share should be what they want to receive, and not just what we want to share. Many times, in our online meetings we will see someone come in who really likes to use LinkedIn so they only will post their LinkedIn URL. This person is assuming that everybody loves to use LinkedIn and that everybody is on the LinkedIn social media platform. The people in the room may or may not be using LinkedIn. Therefore, it is important we have a phone number, an email address, and a calendar link so they can book with us immediately. Those who share their calendar links will typically get three times the bookings of appointments than those who do not.

In online meetings it is also important that we keep our camera on so people can see our face as much as possible. If we are having a problem with internet connection, it is true that we can stay online better if we turn our camera off. In that case, we should make a note of that in the conversation chat so people in the room know we are not trying to be rude by keeping our camera off. People are coming into the meeting wanting to get to know, like and trust each other and nobody is getting to know, like and trust an empty, black screen. They will not feel as favorably towards a picture as they would to seeing us and our smiling face. Networking is not for people who are not willing to participate. It is not for voyeurs. It is for networkers.

If we are going to use our picture because our internet isn't working properly, then we need to make sure it is a picture that looks like us. The picture should be recent and not taken ten years ago when we were twenty-five pounds lighter, and we still had hair. Professionals have professional headshots. If your budget will not allow a professional photographer, at least have somebody hold your phone and take that picture in a place that is well lit with a professional looking back drop. Our profile pictures on social media sites as well as our picture on Zoom should be attractive. We should look professional. A collared shirt is preferable to a deep dive down to our navel. We all need to take a long look at our pictures and decide if we would hire the person in the reflection in the mirror.

People are judgmental. We might like to believe we are not one of those people and that we are all in a very tolerant society. However, there are enough judgmental people in the world to make this a common rule. As a business owner, we want people to buy from us. We do not have time to explain why we are the way we are when they are only looking at something like a picture. They're not going to come back and ask for more details. So, put your best foot forward with a great picture of you.

I have met people who said things like they only want to work with those who have tattoos because they have tattoos. I have met others who only wanted to work with people who had pink hair because they have pink hair. I am sure we have all met people who wanted to give special preferential treatment to those who come from the same cultural or religious background. In reality, these are niche markets. There are pros and cons to niche markets and if we are new to business, there are more cons than pros. We need sales or we go out of business. We should not chase away a willing buyer.

Imagine I am holding a standard 8.5 x 11 blank piece of paper. Now imagine I said I do not want to do business with men. To represent my target market, I am now going to take my paper, tear it in half, and throw away half of the potential buyers. I now have only half of the piece of paper left. I am now going to continue and say I don't want to do business with women who wear dresses. So now I tear off another chunk of my paper which I will throw away. And then I will say I don't want to do business with anyone who wears earrings. And that is going to take what I have left and chop it in half again. The smaller my piece of paper gets, the more focused my niche market is. Soon there is nobody who I can do business with because I have made up my mind that I only do business with a certain kind of person from a certain place who has the same values as I do. Good luck with that! As that piece of paper grows smaller, so will the bank account.

What I have found is that when a business is younger than five years old, or if the business owner is struggling to make more sales, narrowing the target market is not a good course of action. Try to be specific in a description of an avatar of who you would like to do business with, but do not undervalue anyone. Opportunities abound in inclusivity.

We want to have a great big "OPEN FOR BUSINESS" sign over our lives just like we would hang an open sign on our business door. Whether we are online or in-person, we want to be open for business.

How Can We Make Ourselves More Approachable?

In an online business meeting, it is just as important as it is in an in-person meeting to have only one ask. If we are trying to get people to listen to our podcast and that is super important to us, then that should be our one ask. As we share the link, we should ask them to go to the link and click on it right now so that it is open in a window after the meeting is over. It becomes a placeholder reminder for them to visit. If we want everybody in the meeting to subscribe to our YouTube channel, then that should be our one "ask." Share the link as we are talking and ask everybody in the room to go and open that YouTube channel right now and hit the subscribe button while we wait. That will help get it done.

If on the other hand you want them to book a one-on-one appointment with us in the meeting, then we should share our calendar link as we are talking and ask them to hit that calendar link while we are talking and to go to it right now and book an appointment with us.

We never ask for two things in the same sixty-second infomercial because you will get nothing twice as fast as the time it took for you to ask for two things. Have only one "ask" per meeting.

Online Meeting Tips

- Look for meetings where the chat lines are open to talk to people.

- Avoid pep rallies and time wasters.

- Practice your infomercial to be on point and perfectly timed.

- Have your contact information ready to copy and paste and have it ALL ready.

- The feed is moving so repost if new people are coming in but do not monopolize the feed.

- Have only one ask.

- Book one-on-one meetings on the spot using a calendar link. Doing the booking now means my next step in the follow-up process is done.

- Don't limit your customer pool. Inclusion matters.

Want to try out an online networking meeting this week?

Check out the Introductions Meeting on Thursday

https://cibnconnect.com/introduction-sign-up

"Book a meeting from the meeting. If you don't book that second meeting, the first meeting was only a social call. It wasn't a real meeting."

~Kerry George

CHAPTER EIGHT

FOLLOW-UPS THAT WORK

Have you ever had a sales appointment where they did not buy from you the first time you met? If that has happened to you, it is normal. The reality is that we need to show people what we are selling more than once, and they must hear our message more than once to go from being a prospect to being a buyer. Prior to the pandemic, marketing experts were telling us it would take seven to fourteen touches to get a sale. With the pandemic, everyone began taking everything online and we began to get bombarded with increasingly more online messaging. With this shift, it is now more commonly accepted that it takes thirty to sixty touches to turn a new prospect into a sale. That is a lot of touching. Without automation it would be a mammoth and impossible task.

SALES IS NOT AN EVENT. IT IS A PROCESS

Having a sales process is more important today than it has ever been in the history of business. The reality is that most business owners do not have a sales process clearly mapped out. They may never have even taken time to write down the steps in their sales funnel. These are the steps that take a person from that first touch into the place where they become a buyer. Most of us would have more than one funnel on the go. For example, if we are buying Facebook ads and we are using a landing page where we offer a free download, we may get 1000 people taking our offer. That would be the step they take at the top of our funnel. Next, we are going to be asking them to do something. Those who take this step moving down through the funnel are potential buyers. Perhaps, we will invite them to take part in our free five-day challenge. 500 people may take part in the challenge, but only 350 of them end up in our private Facebook group. Out of that number only 180 of those people watch our daily Facebook Lives that go into the group while the challenge is running. On the third day of the challenge, we start to make our offer and by the end of the challenge we have made 12 sales of $2000 each. If the initial marketing cost was $4000 And we made $24,000 in sales, those may be acceptable numbers to us if we don't have a lot of additional overhead.

USING FUNNELS

Each part of the process above was a step in the funnel, and this was just one funnel that was operating in this business. It looks like this.

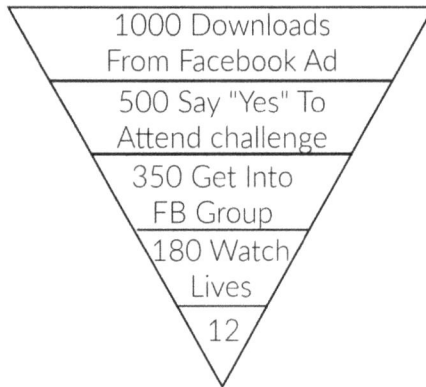

We may have another funnel where people sign up for our webinar. We run ads on Google which is the step at the top of the funnel, and we have 1000 people click through. The free offer we use to bring them in is the webinar itself and 300 people sign up. Only 100 of those who respond attend the webinar, but we do get all 300 onto the email list. As we run the webinar, we close 10 deals on the spot for our $2000 program. There may be a follow-up process with those who attended the webinar and 12 more sales come in from the attendees over the next few weeks. These are all part of our second funnel. By running the webinar repeatedly, and by tracking the amount of money spent on ads that got people into the webinar, we should be able to determine how well our marketing is doing, as well as our cost of lead acquisition.

Our second funnel would look like this:

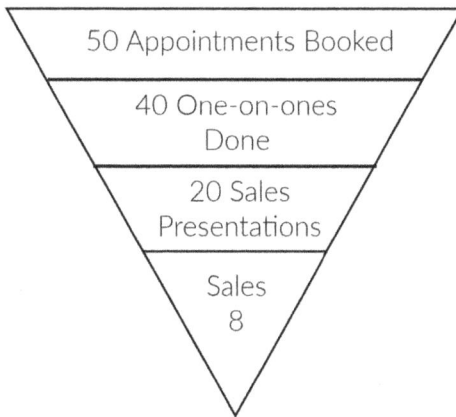

We can use a well-written funnel to give us the data we need to determine the effectiveness of our marketing. When we get one of our funnels to produce leads that convert, we can turn up the volume and scale our business. Looking at the two funnels we created so far, we may determine that the Google ads with the webinar are converting better than the first funnel. This may mean it is a better process and that might be because there is follow-up happening with the attendees after the webinar. It may mean the Facebook funnel needs tweaking. It is likely we can get a better conversion, but without data we shoot in the dark and we never get ahead. By using funnels, we now know which method needs work.

NETWORKING CAN ALSO GIVE US FUNNELS

How does putting people through a funnel work with networking? Networking produces three separate funnels that produce data we can track. There will be a Sales Funnel, a Referral Funnel, and a Collaborating Partner Funnel.

What if we put the people we see in meetings at the top of each of our funnels? Remember our Facebook marketing funnel? We put all the responders to our offer in the top of our funnel. Those who clicked through and took the bait were at the top level of our Google funnel as well. We did not count the thousands of people who noticed the ad on the side of the screen, but they did not click through. Those are impressions.

If we are comparing apples to apples, we should put the number of people who booked an appointment with us at the top of our networking funnels. Those who heard us at the meeting who did not book time with us are impressions, not leads. Therefore, inviting people to a one-on-one meeting with us is that first step of getting them into the funnel.

Networking can potentially be three funnels operating at the same time because we may be putting actual prospects into the top of the funnel as we attend our meetings or when we may be asking the members of the networking group to be bringing us referrals for the people that we want to meet with, or there could be a third funnel for Collaborating Partners.

As we attend networking meetings and as we do one-on-one meetings we are sorting into three silos like this:

1. We meet potential clients who will buy from us directly. These names will go into our Sales Funnel. These people could become buyers.

2. Some people will not be our ideal clients at all. They may lack interest or the budget to buy, however they may have one good lead for us. That is a single referral given by a trusted person and we would call this a warmed-up lead.

3. Collaborating Partners bring a third funnel into play. These are not people who bring us one referral each. These are people that we build special relationships with because their clients are our clients. A Collaborating Partner has our exact target market, but they sell something different than us. When we win the Collaborating Partner over to not only "like" us but to also "know" and "trust" us they can feed us three to five leads each and every month.

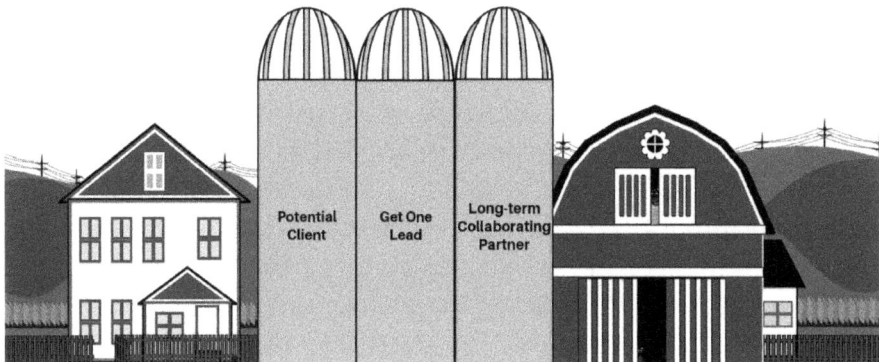

Potential Client | Get One Lead | Long-term Collaborating Partner

We ask questions to prospects we determine which of the silos that they will land in. Good questions break them into silos and this determines what the funnel will look like under the silo. Asking for a meeting is just the first step in the funnel. There may be 50 people who said "yes" this month, but we need to remember that not all will show up for the one-on-one. Track all these numbers to see how well your funnels are working.

THE ONE-ON-ONE IS STEP TWO IN OUR THREE NETWORKING FUNNELS

In our prospecting funnel we need to have clear definitions of steps which are going to lead to the sale. A one-on-one meeting is where we are going to get to know them better and it's where we're going to win them over to like us and trust us more. This is our qualifying step in our funnel. It is where we sort our prospects into one of three buckets. Is this person a potential buyer? Are they a one-time referrer? Or could they become a Collaborating Partner?

One of the most common misconceptions in networking is that a one-on-one meeting should convert immediately to a sale. It does not. If I am selling a $2000 product, it is very unlikely I'm going to be able to sell it to somebody I just met at a networking meeting. Even if my ask is only $100, it may take more than one attempt. The first reason for doing a one-on-one with a prospect is to determine if they are in our target market and if they have the budget to buy from us. The secondary reason is providing the opportunity for them to get to know, like and trust us so they will be a referral source for us. The third reason for this meeting is to see if we can add value to them and their business. These are not in order of priority. Each of these reasons is important. They should be part of every one-on-one meeting to create high-value networking experiences and to make our networking funnels work for us.

We want to use the one-on-one meeting to get to know the person better, too. It is a key part of building a professional relationship. During this meeting we want to talk about who they are. What do they do? What kind of a product or services are they offering? And what kind of client or target market are they trying to reach? A good conversationalist should be able to gather these

pieces of intel in fifteen minutes. Then it is our turn. Should we just jump on them immediately and try to sell them our stuff? Chances are that won't work well, so we will follow the same pattern. We will answer some of the same questions that we just asked them. We will tell them who we are and what we do and why we are so awesome. We will give them some great tips on what to do, but we won't tell them how to do it themselves without us. We should suggest one intriguing solution to their challengers and allude to the fact that we have more solutions.

If we feel this person would be a perfect customer for us, the best course of action would be to book an appointment where we are next going to show them our product or service. We should offer to provide a customized solution that will be revealed on the next appointment. The next appointment will be the sales presentation.

If a sales presentation takes 45 minutes, we definitely do not want to stuff this into the 15 minutes we have left in our one-on-one. Sales conversion will be zero if our sales presentation is not done properly. We need to use a script and stick to the script, so we know what's working. If we are winging it in every appointment, we will not know when it went right and when it went wrong. We take out the guesswork by creating a script to use every time we have a one-on-one.

It's our job to ask lots of questions. Remember that the person who asks the most questions is the one who is in control of the interview. Write out the questions you commonly ask during a one-on-one that help you determine if this person is a prospect, or a referrer, or if they may be a Collaborating Partner. Ask the same questions of each person you meet with one-on-one. Their answers will move them into one of three funnels: the Sales Funnel, the Referral Funnel, or the Collaborating Partner Funnel. Each funnel has a different process that should be clearly mapped out in advance and followed every time we have a one-on-one.

A professional networker should also take this opportunity to find out if this person is a paid member in our networking organization. Paid members build long term relationships, and they have more accountability to each other. If we want them to buy from us, refer to us, or become a Collaborating Partner with us, we will want them to be part of the same group, so we see them regularly. Guests seldom build long term relationships with anyone after a one-time visit to a group. Members will learn our product and repeat our story. Members will be more invested in our success. Ask if they are a member and encourage them to join the group. Those who have invested time and money in the group are more likely to invest time and money into us, and we will also get to pitch to them every week if we take a moment to ask them to join.

THE SALES PRESENTATION IS STEP THREE IN THE FIRST SALES FUNNEL

If we do not have time to do a proper sales presentation and it looks like this person is potentially in our target market, the thing to do next is to book the time to do a real sales presentation. That would be the next step in this first Networking Sales Funnel.

If we give them information about our product or service before we book the appointment, then there is no need to book an appointment with us because they already know everything and they're going to decide before they have the appointment. That is not conducive to a strong bottom line for our business. Therefore, we need to keep our conversation light. We will talk about who we are and what our values are, more than sharing the products and services we offer. If we feel they are in our target market and if we feel they have the budget to make a purchasing decision, we should ask them if they have 45 minutes right now to do the presentation, or if you should rebook it at a better time.

The sales presentation deserves an appointment with a designated time for doing the sales presentation.

This one action will double your results from your networking experiences. Make the appointment.

Delivering the sales presentation is the next step. If we are with a company that provides a sales presentation for us, then we should use it. Someone has already done the marketing research and they know what works, so we should do it one hundred times before we try to recreate the wheel. If we do it three times and it does not work, there is no point complaining to anybody because that's not enough data to tell if the problem is us, or if the problem is the presentation. When we do it one hundred times, we will have data on the number of sales we have made. With data we can refine our process and we can make our presentation better. Winging it is not effective. Do you remember that in the movies nobody remembers the wing man? We only remember the one that is leading, and the one who is successful. To become successful, we need to use a plan and follow the plan.

If we are an entrepreneur who has built our own business, then it is highly likely we will not have a sales process that has been built for us. This means we will have to create a step-by-step procedure in support of growing our business. We will need the data to be able to tell what works for us, and if we are ever going to hire a salesperson, we will want to know what is most likely to work for them. We must create a script we follow every time when making our sales presentation. Your results from the consistent use of a script can be tracked. The script can be tweaked, and most importantly, it can be duplicated by others. We will not have a scalable business or a saleable business if you are not using scripts.

A SCRIPT FOR THE SALES PRESENTATION

Start by asking relevant questions to help determine what the prospect needs. Ask questions before offering advice. Once we feel we understand the customer's situation, we can offer one or two high value solutions

to show them we do know what we are talking about. If our product or service is under $500, we may want to do the full presentation right now and go for the close. Closing is asking for the sale and being ready to accept payment. Not everybody says "yes" the first time the closing question is asked. We need to ask for the sale at least three times.

If our product or service is over $500 you may want to consider having a next step presenting a proposal for them. After we have offered a couple of high-value solutions, we should ask if we can take the information, they have provided to us back to our office to create a special proposal customized for their needs and suited to solving the problems they identified in our question time. If they agree, book the appointment on the spot. Remember that booking an appointment from an appointment is a good practice. When we have a meeting without booking a meeting, it is like we never had a meeting at all. We will do less chasing after those who ghost us if we book the appointment while we are in the meeting.

When a prospect agrees to meet us to hear our proposal in one week's time, we are looking at a strong likelihood of landing that client. People do not generally show up for a proposal meeting if they are not genuinely interested in the proposal.

THE DELIVERY OF THE PROPOSAL IS THE NEXT STEP IN THE SALES FUNNEL

The proposal is the next step in our Sales Funnel. Thought and preparation should go into our proposal. We should show up with a document to go over. This should NEVER be sent to your prospect in advance. Once they have the information in their hands, there is no need for a meeting. This one action kills more sales than any other action. **Deliver the proposal in person or through an online Zoom meeting and make sure there is time set aside to go over the whole thing.**

There should be some statistics and some fast facts, but do not go on too long. Remember those choleric people. They want fast facts, and they want us to look organized. We have covered a lot of material in the one-on-one and in the sales presentation. Right now, we will offer a three-sentence summary reminding them of the problem they have and preparing them to hear our customized solution. The more prepared we are in our proposal, the easier the sale will become. Again, this should be a scripted activity. We don't wing our proposals. Winging it is for KFC, it is not an effective sales process.

80% of the people who meet with us for a second meeting and who know they are coming to look at a proposal are likely to purchase if we are ready to receive payment. If they are not closing, then we need to go over the process and examine it carefully and practice the steps with a colleague to give us feedback. This is a solid plan that should bear measurable results.

THE FOLLOW-UP FUNNEL STEP

The next step in our funnel is the follow up. Did they buy? A buyer needs our followed up. Our buyer is a great person to ask for referrals right after they bought while they are feeling warm and fuzzy and in the honeymoon stage. It is a missed opportunity where we could be losing thousands of dollars each year if we skip this step. We can refer to the Referral Funnel for the next steps in this process.

If they did not purchase, then our next follow-up step is to bring some current information. We should book the appointment for the follow-up while we are in the proposal presenting meeting. Never say, "I will get back to you next week," because that will not happen. I am reminded of the quote by Randy Travis: "The road to hell is paved with good intentions."

Script your follow up. What is the added information you have for them? Show them why this would make a difference. Once again, ask for the sale three separate times in three separate ways. The gold is in the follow up. You are three feet from the gold. Keep digging. If they do not buy, ask for referrals just like you would from a new buyer and book the next follow up meeting. If they say they will consider it in the spring, take out your calendar and book the meeting for the spring. Never leave a meeting without booking the next meeting or you wasted your time in the first meetings.

THE NETWORKING SALES FUNNEL

This is what the Networking Sales Funnel looks like without a proposal step. If we were selling a product less than $500, the proposal may not be necessary.

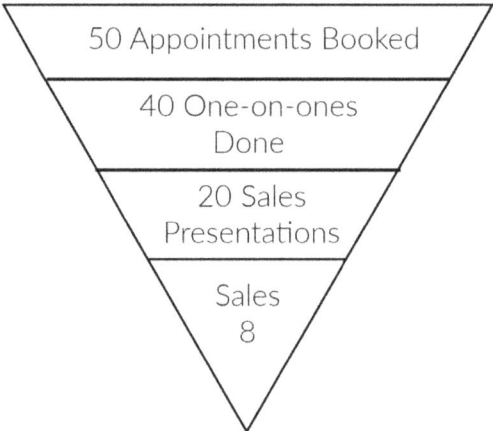

50 Appointments Booked

40 One-on-ones Done

20 Sales Presentations

Sales 8

This is what the Networking Sales Funnel looks like if a proposal step was necessary:

```
\                                           /
 \        50 Appointments Booked          /
  _____/
   \          40 One-on-ones            /
    \             Done                 /
     _____/
      \         20 Sales             /
       \      Presentations         /
        _____/
         \         15            /
          \     Proposals       /
           _____/
            \     Sales      /
             \      7       /
              _____/
               \         /
                \       /
                 \     /
                  \   /
                   \ /
                    V
```

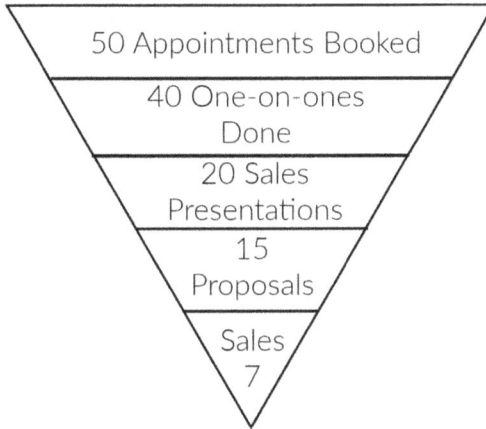

Asking for Referrals is the Next Step in the Referral Funnel

Most people go networking because they see it as a useful source of referrals. When they don't get referrals, they become frustrated, and they often blame the people in their network. The truth is networking works well when we work our nets properly. Amateurs often struggle with things that professionals find simple. The real difference between these two perspectives is that one has no plan or process, while the other has a solid process they use consistently.

Getting referrals is simple when we have a process.

If we don't ask for referrals, we won't get any. If we casually ask for one referral in a less than powerful way at the end of the meeting, we will not get any. If we ask for only one referral, we will rarely get one. Why not ask for more than one to double or triple the odds? Why not ask for ten?

Think about it. If we just spent forty minutes with someone who is never going to buy from us, what do we have to lose by asking? He already said "No." We are not going to lose the business he might have given us today. There is nothing to lose by asking. We want to script our referral ask just like we script every other step in the sales funnel.

Years ago, we encountered an insurance salesperson who reported he did about ten times the volume of all the insurance salespeople combined in the entire business network. We invited him to our office and asked him what his secret was. He was happy to show us. It came down to one thing he did, and others would not take the time to do. He had a list of ten questions where he asked for specific referrals. He went through these questions with every buyer on the delivery day of their policy, and he used it in the one-on-one with the person who was not going to be a buyer. If he met for a proposal meeting with someone who ended up not buying, he brought out these ten questions and asked for ten referrals.

He was a professional networker, and he treated the process like a pro. He also enjoyed the commission cheques of a pro. While some people in his industry had a problem getting one sale in the network in an entire year, he often made over $30,000 in commissions per quarter from only attending one networking meeting a week.

He asked things like:

1. Who do you know who recently had a baby?

2. Who do you know that sold their home and upgraded to a larger home?

3. Do you know anyone who bought a house about four years ago?

4. Do you know any working couples that have two or more

children and who are struggling to make ends meet?

5. Do you know anyone who was laid off from a high paying position in the last year?

6. Who do you know that likes to travel?

7. Do you have a friend who has a job and has complained that they are paying too much in taxes?

8. Do you know a business owner who has three to ten employees?

9. Do you know anyone with kids that have just started college?

10. Do you know anyone in their forties who is worried about their retirement?

He had solutions for the problems that each of these people would have, so he carefully worded his questions to make a person think of someone they knew. He had the questions on a sheet of paper that he would place in front of them. He would then hand them a pen and ask them to write just the first name of whoever came into their mind as he read each question out loud to them. Did you hear what I just said?

He did not give them a list, ask them to look it over and get back to him if they thought of someone. He did not use a lame approach like that because it is useless and does not work. He read the questions aloud. Yes, I am repeating myself. Why?

I have worked with entrepreneurs for more than a decade and I can feel some of you skipping through to the end because this is uncomfortable. People often resist doing what is uncomfortable so STOP. READ THAT AGAIN.

He read it aloud while they had the paper in front of them, and the pen in their hands. People dutifully took the pen and started writing. What if you could do this on your next one hundred appointments? Would your lead list explode? Would your business soar?

Once he was done going through the questions, he asked them to put the last name of each person on the paper. Then he showed them a simple statement of how he was going to contact each of the people on their lists. He explained that he would say their friend mentioned them to him. He would add that he asked the referrer for their phone number He commonly got ten referrals at once, and sometimes more. He never got less than three referrals.

This is a valuable process for a professional networker. To practice this process, what are ten questions you could ask for your industry? Write them down right now and make this part of your sales process this week.

THE REFERRAL FUNNEL

As we look at the Referral Funnel, we will see that the top three lines in the funnel are the same as the Sales Funnel. That is because we are working from the same 50 appointments. During our one-on-one discussion with our prospect, we will make a decision based on how they answered our questions whether they are our ideal candidate for a purchase or not. When they do not land in our target market, we cease selling. There is no need to set up a sales presentation with them. If we cannot make a sale, we should aim for getting referrals. Notice that a proper follow-up with scripted questions may produce 40 or more referrals. Add those to the sales that came in and remember that a warmed-up referral will have at least twice the closing ratio of any other kind of lead we can get—anywhere.

This is what our Referral Funnel will look like:

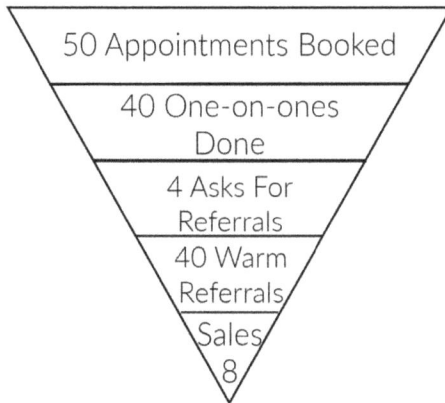

```
50 Appointments Booked
   40 One-on-ones
        Done
    4 Asks For
     Referrals
    40 Warm
    Referrals
     Sales
       8
```

THE COLLABORATION FUNNEL

Our third funnel is the Collaboration Funnel. This is a professional networking concept, and it requires explanation and strategy, so I have committed the entire next chapter to this subject. However, I will show you the funnel diagrams to whet your appetite.

When the Collaboration Strategy is employed, the funnel will look like this in Month One.

Month One may not appear to be that exciting, but we should look carefully at the concept because these three referrals are not the ordinary run of the mill referrals. These referrals are clients of our Collaborating Partner who have already spent substantial funds with them. They are buyers, not tire kickers. The closing ratio on these leads will be about 80%. In our diagram, we are using a closing ratio of two out of three, and in comparison, our other diagrams are showing a closing ratio of one out of five. Their trusted advisor and friend recommended that we are the answer for their problems, and he has lined up the appointment with the expectation they will become our client.

Let's have a look at what this one month of business has brought us already.

Networking Sales Funnel	Referral Funnel	Collaboration Funnel
50 appointments booked	50 appointments booked	50 appointments booked
40 one on ones done	40 one on ones done	40 one on ones done
20 sales presentations	4 asks for referrals	1 collaboration partner
15 proposals	40 warm referrals	3 warm referrals
Sales 7	sales 8	sales 2

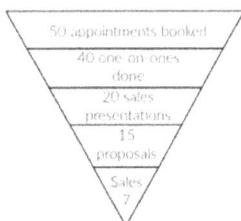

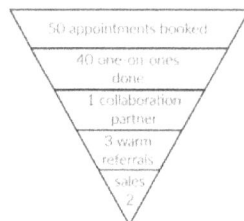

Using the funnel where one would be using the additional step of offering proposals, we can see we are working with the same 50 appointments booked over one month. That is about 12 or 13 appointments a week. If one does not want to work as hard, simply dial down the numbers. If one wants bigger results, then we add more appointments booked.

In this example these 50 appointments bring in seven sales from those that were in the networking meetings and eight more sales came in from the referrals. There were only two sales from the Collaborating Partner this month, but they were easier to close, and it is also possible they bought our biggest packages because they were in the market, they had the budget, and they came from someone who highly recommended us as the professional in our industry. This is a good month for most people. A total of 17 sales and we were offering a $2000 service in our example, so that would be a $34,000 month assuming that our typical initial closing ratio is one out of seven and our referral rate is 100% or more when those referrals come from buyers.

Would I guarantee this? If I were the salesperson in the scenario, I would guarantee an even greater result, however I am not the salesperson in question. You are. So, I have a few questions for you. Would you guarantee you would book 50 appointments from your networking? That means you will have to attend three to ten meetings a week in a network that allows you to book appointments on the spot. Will you put in the hours? Will you create a process and script it for every step of your sales process? Will you treat your business as seriously as I treat my business?

There are many things that could get in the way of success, but the biggest "but" in the room is the one we sit on. Will we get off it and do the work?

These are my numbers, and they are the numbers I have found to be consistent with what most people do. I suggest you look at these funnels and recreate them for your business. Start dropping in the numbers for appointments as you complete them. Start sorting and creating processes. It will change the very nature of your business and it will show you exactly what you can expect as you increase the number of appointments you set.

Over time, the results become extremely exciting. Stay tuned as we show you in the next chapter what this will look like over the next year as we bring on more Collaborating Partners. The leads we get from Collaborating Partners are easier to close and they come more readily to us. With the right Collaborating Partners, we don't need to rely on what comes out of the networking meetings as much. It becomes steady, predictable, and much less work. This may become the last sales growth strategy that is ever needed in your business!

To refine your follow-up script and to improve overall confidence and sales ability, you will want to take part in the SALES PRO program at CIBN Connect.

Overcome your fear of selling and the bad habits that keep you from success.

We turn introverts and grandmothers into sales superstars in this program!

https://www.cibn.club/join-sales-pro-page

CHAPTER NINE

The $150,000/Year Collaboration Strategy

The Collaboration Strategy is incredibly effective. People will compare this to a Joint Venture Partnership but as we begin, I want to explain that a Collaboration Strategy is not a Joint Venture Partnership. These are two vastly different things.

Joint Venture Partnership

A Joint Venture Partnership usually implies we are going to work with one person, and we are both going to financially benefit from the sale of a product or service. Perhaps I have a large email list, and my JV Partner has a product. I agree to send out emails to my email list and in exchange for doing that, my JV Partner is going to share revenue that comes from the sale of his product.

Another example is a marketer who wants to get new clients. He wants to do a Joint Venture Partnership with accountants. He leaves copies of his book that shows him as an industry leader with his accountant and encloses a brochure. The brochure contains a code that is unique to the accountant. When he gets a call originating from his brochure, he offers a special value-added product or service, and asks for the code. The code tells him exactly which accountant handed out his book to this prospect. When one of these people becomes a client, he sends a 20% referral reward to the referring accountant.

Collaboration Strategy

Joint Venture Partnerships are common practices in business, and they can be effective, but they are not collaborations. A Collaboration Strategy is something that any business owner could do, but most never think of it. This strategy would work in any business network; however, it works best in a group where the members are aware of it. When we try to follow these steps in a free group that does not charge membership fees, the members may not understand why people who are not buying from them are requesting a second and third appointment. If we are part of a networking group that encourages collaboration and abundance instead of competition, this is easier. People who concentrate on collaboration are not worried about competition, or who owns what seat in their club. They are looking for ways to create win/win situations. Collaboration will come more naturally to members of this group.

One advantage of the Collaboration Strategy is that we do not need to have a large email list to get started. If we have some existing clients, the implementation of the strategy could be easier, but it is not impossible for a new business owner who has not made a single sale yet.

Before we can begin our first step, it is necessary to decide who our target market is. A Collaborating Partner is going to have a remarkably similar target market, so we must be clear on who is in our target market.

Knowing our target market is important for any marketing that we would be doing for our business. Over our years of networking and business experience we have met many people who have said very silly things like, "I could sell my product to anybody." "My service is good for everybody." "Everyone should be using what I have." "My skin care product is good for anybody with skin."

These statements are completely ineffective in an infomercial, because when I hear that you are looking for ANYBODY it makes me think of absolutely NOBODY. If an entrepreneur were going to buy advertising and WE had this philosophy, we would spend thousands of dollars and miss our target every time.

How Do We Find Our Target Market?

We look at our previous customers if we have any. What do they have in common? Are most of them women between the ages of 40 and 55? Are they couples with children? Are they 55-year-old business owners? When we look at our previous customers, we will usually find a common link that runs through most of them. That commonality should give us some clues about who our target market is.

We may also want to look at who we enjoy doing business with. Are we trying to get away from working with a certain group of people? Are we trying to get into a new market? We could build an avatar for our perfect client. What would they wear? How old would they be? What kind of car do they drive? What do they like to do with their spare time? Do they share a common hobby? What problem do we solve for them?

I have a word of caution in establishing our target markets: this should make sense. New business owners often struggle with where to start, so they will pick a lofty goal that sounds good to them, but does it make sense?

I once had a salesperson who was new to our business network and who was struggling to figure out who he should target with his service. One day he came bounding into my office full of excitement that he had found his ideal target market! I was thrilled for him until he explained the idea to me. Then I was not thrilled. Why? He was picking a large market out of a hat. It was something he thought sounded good. He had decided he was going to focus on selling to the LGBT community. After hearing him out, I asked a few questions. I asked if he was gay. He replied, "No." I asked if he had a close friend or family member who was gay. He said, "No," and then he admitted he did not know a single person from the LGBT community. By this point I was wondering why he thought this was a promising idea. He said he thought it was a market that was not being served in the business community. I had not done any research on the subject so I could not agree or disagree with his logic. I have friends who are gay, so I thought I could start my research by asking their opinions, but I continued to question him. Why did he feel he should focus on this demographic of the population? He then informed me he felt it would be easy because he could go to the annual pride parade and see who had floats. Those who had floats might have the budget for his program.

Although I could see where he was going, it was a flawed logic. The program he was selling was for business owners only. In fact, only small business owners would be interested, not the owners of large companies. His products held zero interest for employees. I asked him if he knew how many floats in the parade represented small business where he would be able to contact the business owner easily. He had no answer for that, so I opened YouTube, and we had a look at the recordings of the parade from the previous year. Guess what we found? One out of thirty floats in the parade were representing small business owners. Was this a good market for him?

If he were from the LGBT community, or if he had close friends and associates from the community, he may have been onto something. Still, the leads he would need would most likely come from other members of the community. We did have members in our business network who were from the LGBT community, so I referred him to them to conduct further research. They also discouraged him.

He is not the only one I have seen make these mistakes in business. I have met people who wanted to sell things to churches who were not Christians. Good luck with that! I was a Pastor for 14 years, and the first question any Pastor, board member, or senior leader in any church will ask a salesperson is where they stand in their faith. Before we get all judgemental about this, consider it carefully. Are we not attracted to the people who are most like us? Don't we want to be surrounded by people who think like us? Even if we are the most open-minded people in the universe, do we not want to be surrounded by other open-minded people?

Sales go easier when we find people who relate to us. Sales do not come easily when we first must educate our prospects or change their mind about something. If we are in sales, then we need to focus on the thing we sell. We don't need to have all these other conversations first, so avoid them. Stick to the point. We should start with the crowd that naturally wants to go with us.

Don't leave anyone out who comes through the door but target a group that makes sense. I have seen women who decided to focus on selling their coaching service to mothers, but they were not mothers themselves. This made no sense. They struggled every day to relate to the few clients they find, and found it was arduous work to get more. We encouraged these coaches to focus on women who are working without being specific if they were mothers or not. Their business began to soar because it felt more natural to them. Soon they had professional women who were mothers, grandmothers, and others who had no children at all. They could easily relate to professional women because they were professional women.

I have seen women who wanted to sell only to women when their products were also great for men. They thought they related best to women but when we looked at their previous customers, they discovered that 60% of the purchases were made by men for themselves or the women in their lives. Why were they focusing on women only? It was because of a feeling they had, and it made no sense. With further investigation we were able to determine the common thread of one gal's customers was not gender. It was persons in professional careers. 90% of her clients were doctors, lawyers, and executives. When she realized this, she was able to change her marketing to be more effective and we were able to find excellent collaborators for her.

Who is your ideal target market? What is their age? Who are they? Where do they live? Where do they play? Can we picture them? Could we build an avatar? What do they have in common with each other?

Once we know who is in our target market, we can begin looking for a Collaborating Partner who has exactly the same target market as ours. It would be ideal if they sold something to this target market that is different from what we sell.

If I have 40 clients who have paid me $2000 to buy my service in the last year and you have 40 clients who have paid you $2500 each in the last year, and we both sell to the same target market, we have something in common and that could make us great collaborating partners. If we know, like, and trust each other, collaboration could work. The know, like and trust part is the kicker.

I have met people who attend only one or two networking meetings and quickly discover there is somebody in the room who would have a remarkably similar target market to them. They set up a one-on-one appointment and think they will immediately get leads from the other person. That is not likely to happen. The reason? You and this person have not established a relationship with each other or with us as a networking organization. We have not gotten to the place where the know, like and trust factor has happened. We are missing that magic ingredient for building a relationship over time. Time and more importantly, time spent together are the ingredients of real relationships. In one meeting we are only establishing "like." It takes more meetings to get to the "know" and "trust" factors.

Who do we really know, like and trust? Are they the people who we have met with a few times or many times? Think about colleagues who you know, like and trust. Do you not have a relationship with them? Why would investigating the possibility of using the collaborative strategy be any different? How do we make friends and influence people? How will we win them over to know us, and like us and trust us and still have effective use of our time? We could wait for this to magically happen somehow, or we could just do the work and make it happen. Which would you prefer? Which would have measurable results?

What if we had a process to go deeper with a new acquaintance so they would feel they know us, and like us, and trust us faster? What if we used this method on a handful of people, instead of trying to meet with 100 new people this month? What if we found three people in that handful who started to know us, like us and trust us enough to give us three warm, quality leads each month? Would that improve your bottom line? And what if we could find five people over the next three months who would be willing to give us three to five warmed-up leads every month? What would five warm leads every month, month after month do for our business? What if these leads were exactly in our target market and they had been told wonderful things about us? What if they were recommended to move quickly to do business with us because we are terribly busy, professional people who get things done? What if these people were known buyers who were already working with the referral source? Would these things help?

EXPLORING COLLABORATION

These questions tell you what a Collaborating Partner would be like. Do you see the difference between this and a Joint Venture Partner? A Collaborating Partner is somebody with whom we have built a relationship. We do not have to take years to build this kind of relationship, but we do have to meet more than once. I'm going to show you how to do it in four meetings. Each of these meetings will be one hour in length. We could add one Collaborating Partner a month for five months, or we can go faster. It is up to us.

COLLABORATION MEETING #1

In a previous chapter we talked about what to do in a one-on-one meeting. The first step is to script our one-on-one event, so we do it exactly the same every time. **The questions we ask should determine if this prospect is going to become a client, if they are going to be giving us a few referrals, or if they**

are qualified to become a Collaborating Partner. We want to find out what their needs are, who they serve, and if they have exactly the same target market as ours with clients of their own who they could refer to us.

If the answers to the questions determine they fall into the category of a client or a one-time referrer, then we will follow the steps in our Sales Funnel or our Referral Funnel as they were outlined in Chapter Eight.

If your questions determine this person has the same target market as us and they offer a service that is complimentary to our own clients, then we will want to book another meeting to get to know them better. We should book this meeting while we are in the one-on-one so we can take this relationship to a new level where it will produce warmed-up leads for both of us sooner as opposed to later.

A Collaborating Partner is of the highest importance. These next meetings should be treated with the greatest of respect. We don't want to miss these appointments or let anything impede the direction of this relationship-building process.

COLLABORATION MEETING #2

In the first meeting, you each spoke about who you are and what you do and what kind of business you have, so we don't want to cover that again. Professional networkers take notes the first time, so there is no need to repeat that information. In this second meeting we want to deepen our relationship, so we are going to ask different questions and we are going to offer different information about ourselves than we did the first time.

Ask questions like, "How did you get started in business?" Telling the story of how their business was created will generally get the person to open up to you in a deeper level. You may then want to share how you got started in your business. Remember, people love you more when they get to talk about themselves. You want to be authentic and share from the heart, but you do not want to monopolize the time. Here are more questions to ask:

1. What is your vision for the future of your business? This question can get people sharing their optimism about their future. It puts them into a dreaming mode. They will often tell us things they haven't even shared with the people who are closest to them. We will want to tell them about the vision we have for our business, too, but briefly. This is our opportunity to help them get to know you a little bit better. Be mindful of the clock. This meeting is supposed to be about them, not us. We all love to talk about our dreams and goals, but we should be mindful to not overdo it.

2. What is your WHY? Oftentimes when we ask somebody why they do the things they do, they will give you the answer they think sounds good instead of the real answer. Unless they have done some personal growth work, they may not know what their WHY is. The best way to get them to be authentic and give us a "real" answer is for us to go first and provide an example.

Do you know what your WHY is? We will need to know the answer to this question to be effective when we ask someone else.

What is the thing that gets us off the couch to go to another call? What really motivates us? What drives us? Why does it drive us? If our WHY does not make us cry, it likely is not the real reason why we do what we do. A real WHY should invoke some emotion.

When we are asked this question, we may initially be uncomfortable to go that deep and so we will give a shallow answer to the question. We will say something like, "I do this for my kids."

If that is your answer, I would ask you, "Why do you do this for your kids?"

When we ask the question WHY each time somebody answers us, we take them to a newer and deeper level of WHY they do what they do.

The person may answer back that they want to do this for their kids so they will have everything in life they want.

Why?

"Well, because I wouldn't want them to be doing without?"

And I would ask another why?

"Well, because we had to do without when I was a kid, and it was not a very pleasant experience."

Why?

"Well, I remember one time not having shoes to wear to school and it was embarrassing. The kids made fun of me, and I wouldn't want that to happen to my kids."

"Why? How would that make you feel if your kids were doing without, and they were embarrassed because they did not have shoes?"

As you take this person back to that key experience where they intensely feel the pain and the anguish of that moment, they capture the emotion on which they can capitalize. When they are lead further and deeper to find that feeling, the emotion they uncover will impact their outcomes.

We are motivated to take action in response to either pleasure or pain. I think most people would like to be rewarded with something that is pleasurable rather than be on the receiving end of pain. After years of training salespeople, I can affirm that many would say they want to be rewarded for achieving a goal with things like a higher paycheck or a trip to Hawaii. They would promise to do great things for the company if those kinds of compensations were added to the payment plan.

Unfortunately, external rewards for performance may not bring about your desired outcome. You could find that one or two out of a staff of twenty salespeople might be highly motivated and work like crazy to get the trip to Hawaii and the rest would watch them do it. Why? Because some people are motivated by pain; they just don't want to admit it.

It is the pain of not having enough, or the fear of lack, or the memory of something embarrassing that drives people. As we are digging into what is our personal WHY, we will often find that the root of it has something to do with an experience that made us feel badly.

If I said my WHY was because I want to have a good retirement and we dug down deeper into that, we might find I had an experience that was unsavory. My story might reveal I had a close relative who worked well past an acceptable retirement age and died while at work.

Before we start asking people for their WHY, we should know what our WHY is. Do the work. Dig down at least seven questions deep. Why? Why? Why? Why? Why? Why? Why? When we start to feel emotion, we are somewhere near the truth.

In this second meeting we may not want to go so deep with this person that you are both bawling uncontrollably, but we want to get deeper than the first or second level of WHY. We want to hear what their real WHY is because it will tell us more about who they are. It will help us get closer to having a real friendship.

We want to share what our real WHY is because it is a part of ourselves that is deep. Superficial answers keep potential customers on the outside looking in. If we want this person to give us their best leads and their paying customers, we need to go deeper. Nobody is offering that to a stranger.

If this Collaborating Partner is going to give us five high quality referrals a month every month, the chances are good they are going to become a particularly good friend. But the reality is they're not going to give you five referrals a month every month until we have already become friends. These are the kinds of subjects that real friends talk about together. The sooner we initiate these conversations and start to be authentic with one another, the sooner we are going to get to the place where you "know" them, "like" them, and "trust" them completely.

We want to be sure to book the next meeting while we are in this meeting so that you can move on in this relationship. Think about it. Make the next meeting for a week from now. If we were beginning a courtship and we asked a girl out and had an enjoyable time, how long should we wait to get together with her again? If we wait too long, we will fall out of favor. We need to keep this relationship moving forward, so book it now. At the end of the first date, we arrange the next date.

Tell them that next time we are getting together, we are going to be bringing a lead for them and we will be talking about how they are going to approach this person. We should also let them know we would like them to bring one lead for us and we will discuss how to approach their friend or client. This information makes them feel safe and ready for the next step as they are starting to know, like and trust us.

COLLABORATION MEETING #3

Let's say we were feeling great after the second meeting like we were making a new friend. Now we are meeting for the third time and this time we are going to talk about the giving and the receiving of a lead.

One of the reasons people don't give you access to their clients immediately is because they are worried about how we are going to approach that client. They are worried about whether we are going to do something that would embarrass them in front of their client. They are concerned we may ask their client for money their client does not have, or that we may be rude to them or overbearing in our request.

In this third meeting, we are going to put their mind at ease about how you deal with their clients, and we are going to ask them to put our mind at ease about how they are going to deal with the leads we give to them.

Since most people have not taken training on this, you are going to have to lead this conversation. We have a week to get ready and come prepared with one good lead to give our new Collaborating Partner. We should have the contact information ready to give them during this third meeting. We should be ready and willing to send a carbon copied email to them and the person we are referring to them. We will be saying important things about who they are and what they do, and we will highly recommend that the referral books time to meet with our Collaborating Partner right away.

In this third meeting with our Collaborating Partner, we should talk about who this lead is and why you think they would be an ideal candidate to buy their product or service from our Collaborating Partner. We will talk about the problem that your referral has and how our Collaborating Partner is going to solve that problem for them.

Next, we will ask them what their process is with a referral. How long will it take for them to contact the referral? Will they set up a meeting with them right away? Do they have time in their calendar this week to look after this? Will they meet with them one time, or will they meet with them to find out who they are and then put together a proposal and have a second meeting? We should ask if there is anything that they would like us to tell that person.

We will take notes as we ask these questions. If we are taking a whole hour to meet with our Collaborating Partner right now, then we have time to go into our email during this third meeting in front of them and craft the message right there. Read it out to them or have them dictate what we should say.

I would recommend an email to both parties. I might say something like this if my new Collaborating Partner was named Bob.

> Hello Bob and Carol, I wanted to take a minute to introduce the two of you.
>
> Bob and I have recently started doing some business together. He has been explaining the problems he solves for people in your industry, Carol. As we were speaking, I realized that he has the ideal solutions I know you need.
>
> Carol has been a client of mine and a friend for six years. She is excellent at what she does and a professional in her field. She has years of wisdom that she loves to share with others.
>
> I know the two of you are going to benefit from this connection.
>
> Bob, I know how busy you are, but can you please take time to meet with my friend, Carol. I would consider it a personal favor to me.
>
> Thanks.
>
> Your name

I may add specific things in the email like what Carol does for living or what the real problem or solution would be and how this is relevant to them both.

How would you respond if you got an email like this introducing you to someone? Do you see the value of this? Are you aware this kind of a warmed-up referral from a close friend has a closing ratio of 50%? If Bob is sending this to a client who trusts him as a valuable advisor and the referral has been prequalified, the email could have a closing ratio of 80% or more.

How many of these would you like in a month?

This is how a Collaborating Partner sends qualified referrals to their Collaborating Partner. This was only one referral. Once we have set up this referral for our Collaborating Partner, we are now going to ask him to give us one. As we ask, we are going to explain to him what our sales process is and how you are going to approach his friend or client. If he did not bring a referral with him, we are going to ask him an extremely specific question so he can think of somebody to refer to us right now.

For example:

> "Bob I just want to remind you that I help my clients stop spending money needlessly on marketing methods that do not work. Is there anyone you have been working with in the last 12 months who has complained they have spent money on marketing that was not working?"

Do you see how this kind of specific question is more likely to get a result? Once we ask the question it is important to be quiet so Bob can think about what his answer is. Suddenly Bob remembers her name and says, "Yes I have a client named Sally who has had this exact problem!"

Awesome! Now we will tell Bob how we are going to treat Sally as she becomes our client. Then ask him for Sally's email and phone number. We want this even if Bob is going to CC us all in on the same email. We are professionals with a process. We do not want to hunt for the details later and waste time.

Next, we ask Bob to write us an email and to send us a CC on the conversion with Sally. We will ask him to do it now while we are in this third meeting. We will help him to craft the message and hit send.

Now that we have given our Collaborating Partner a warmed-up lead, and he has given us a warmed-up lead, we will want to book our next meeting for two weeks from now.

COLLABORATION MEETING #4

In the fourth meeting you will want to get together to talk about what happened with the one lead they gave you. How did it go?

In some industries we may not be able to give details because you must protect the confidentiality of the client. We can, however, tell Bob we did meet with the lead. We can tell him it was a good meeting, and it was enjoyable getting together with his friend or client. We can tell Bob we expect things to work out, but we can't share the details, or what the investment commitment is. Bob will understand. He just wants to know his referral was a good one and that we are following through with this person who he cares about.

In this fourth meeting we are going to come equipped with three more warmed-up leads for Bob. We are going to go through who they are with him and give him a heads-up about why they would be great clients for him. We will share contact information with Bob so he can do a proper follow-up.

It would be ideal if we sent the warmed-up leads email introducing them to Bob before the meeting. Typically, I would have done it just before I am getting together with Bob, or I would do it immediately after the meeting I have with Bob. I am also going to ask Bob for three warmed-up referrals now. By this time, he is getting comfortable with the process.

Using this process, we have turned Bob into a Collaborating Partner. Each month we should meet with Bob one time, and we should bring with us five leads for Bob. We should come with five questions that will remind Bob of who he could refer to us in case he forgot to prepare for the meeting, and we will leave each of these meetings with five warmed-up referrals from Bob. This one action will dramatically change our bottom line this year.

Imagine a world where you have five friends who give you five warmed-up leads every month and that they are their paying clients who have been prequalified for our product or service. Imagine a world where this happens month after month.

The diagram shows how this would work if we found one Collaborating Partner a month for only five months. In their first thirty days, each Collaborating Partner mentions only three warm leads but in their second month they begin offering five warmed-up leads per month. For many business owners, entrepreneurs, and professionals, this number of leads would dramatically change their lifestyles.

In the previous chapter we discussed a method that would take three networking meetings a week which is twelve hours a month. Then we would add the fifty hours of appointments to go through to arrive at seventeen sales. There would have been additional meetings to deliver proposals. It would have been a remarkably busy, high impact month.

In this scenario by the sixth month, we are bringing in twenty sales, but we are working much less time to get those sales. We got these leads in five meetings that took a total of five hours maximum. As time goes by, we could shorten these meetings to half that time so it would take two and a half hours to collect the leads. Then there are 25 appointments instead of 50 because the quality of these leads and the amounts they would spend is significantly higher.

1ST MONTH

1 Collaboration Partner

3 Warm Referrals

2 Sales

2ND MONTH

2 Collaboration Partners

6 Warm Referrals

4 Sales

3RD MONTH

3 Collaboration Partners

11 Warm Referrals

8 Sales

4TH MONTH

4 Collaboration Partners

16 Warm Referrals

12 Sales

5TH MONTH

5 Collaboration Partners

21 Warm Referrals

16 Sales

6TH MONTH

5 Collaboration Partners

25 Warm Referrals

20 Sales

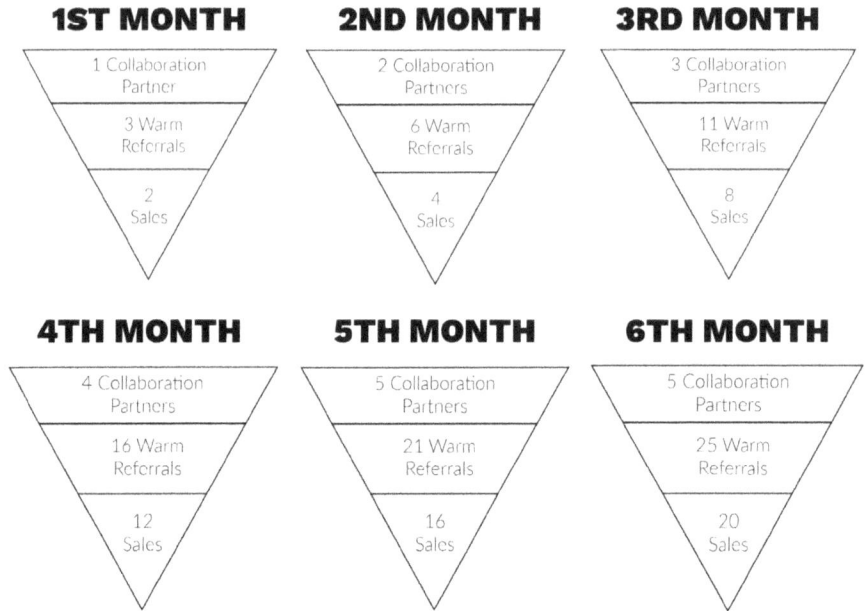

If I were a salesperson who made a $2000 commission on each sale, this would increase my monthly commissions to $40,000 in only six months. The Collaboration Strategy is worthy of time and consideration!

There is additional training available in the CIBN Connect video portal for our Speaker level and Sales Pro members. To find out more about these basic levels of membership check out this link https://www.cibn. club/memberships-usd

CHAPTER TEN

Next Steps Now That You Are A Networking Pro

We have learned a lot about networking. We learned about networking online and we compared that to networking at in-person events. We talked about old-fashioned networking and compared it to modern methods. We covered how to do an infomercial, and what to do in our one-on-one. We discussed sales presentations and we provided the tools on how to build a collaboration team.

So how do we get started? There are all kinds of networking opportunities available to us right now. Every community has networking organizations and clubs that are currently running. What should we be looking for?

Choose A Great Networking Group With These Characteristics

1. **A Business Community**. A business community allows us to do business. If we are not allowed to talk about our business during the meetings, this is not a business community. We can't sit around singing kumbaya hoping that someday we will get to talk about our business. You may still get to do business with members of the group or their connections but it may take more time for it to happen.

What we have to offer in our business needs the opportunity to be freely discussed. This is the most genuine and sincere type of networking. We are there to do business.

Some organizations run with a culture of "business only" without making friends and there is some success with that model. However, from our experience we have discovered that having a community where people care about each other beyond business is beneficial to the growth of every business owner and to their bottom line.

Where the members feel they are like family and they actually do get to know, like and trust each other, there can be a greater reward financially and emotionally. The benefits of belonging to a group that has this blended purpose surpass both the "business only" model and the "feeling good" model.

2. **Emphasis Is On Relationships**. A good networking organization helps people buildpositive and lasting relationships as well as great business relationships and mentoring relationships. Having this skill set may improve our personal and family relationships, too. Training needs to be supplied for this to happen. People don't become better people through osmosis; they need to be informed and they benefit from being led through training. Any organization that is not investing in the progress of its people is not contributing to their growth and improvement.

3. **Few Rules**. There are some organizations that pile the rules on top of the members. They must come early; they must stay late. They must have a referral for someone at every meeting. They pay a fine if they do not have a referral. This type of structure appeals to the analytical personality as described earlier in this book, but everyone else struggles with this model. It feels aggressive and it is problematic to retain members when we are continuously using a stick to keep them in line.

In the rule-oriented network, we work hard for the glory of the organization. We recruit for the network, and we sell for the network, and we leave little time to recruit or sell for our own business. Working on behalf of the network can tire people out and convince them that networking is hard.

The moderators of these types of groups would argue that business owners need to have accountability to each other, and I do not disagree with accountability. However, it should not come in the form of a dictatorship. If we are going to network with people every week, there should be enjoyment in the process. We should not feel like we must be there. We should feel like we want to be there. Inevitably, we will be there a lot longer if we enjoy the experience and it is not a burden to us. Business owners do not need another job and they don't need a boss with a long list of rules.

4. **Fun**. Life is too short to fill our days and weeks with activities that are a drag. Our networking group members should experience some fun. With fun, attendance is easy, and the relationships and the community will flourish.

5. **Membership Fees**. A great organization is not running on volunteerism. It runs with professional staff who get paid and who are doing the work behind the scenes to make the time invested better for all the networking members. We cannot expect that we are going to get this kind of valuable customer service for free.

In a great network there are many moving parts. There are a variety of meetings to attend, training to take, and expertise to avail ourselves of. With all of the events running each week, operating the network is like juggling bowling balls, glass plates and wild cats all at the same time. This means that a team with a system is planning your membership experience from one month to the next. There is a cost to this kind of networking and it should be a fair price that is not going to sink the budget.

There is value in belonging to a network that is working for you. And there is value in being an active member. Networking is the most cost-effective marketing one can buy with the greatest potential for returns, and it is a tax-deductible expense in most countries. It is important for us to weigh if we are getting good value for the dollars being spent.

6. **No Or Very Little Volunteerism**. We are business owners, entrepreneurs and professionals, and we do not have time to be volunteering to run a business network. If we are going to do any helping, it should not be more than fifteen minutes a week. Our time is precious. It is the most precious commodity we have. We cannot give it away for free and expect to reap some reward we can't put our finger on. Real businesses run off data and we expect to have outcomes with data that indicates a return on our investment for the time we commit to a project and for the financial resources we pour into the project.

If we are doing volunteer work, then it should be for a cause we really believe in. What if the inner-city poor were better served with our volunteerism? Our business network should be a profitable business enterprise that can afford staff. How else could they dare to call themselves business leaders? How can they assist the business owners with guidance and training if they do not run a successful enterprise themselves? Any organization to which we pay fees for the purpose of bringing us additional business should practice what they preach. If they require volunteerism and not paying staff, then they are not a real business in my books.

7. **Training**. Is training offered as part of the membership? It is no longer the dark ages.We should have our cake and eat it, too. Why are we spending $10,000 a year on courses? Why are we looking for "experts" to bring us up to date on LinkedIn? If LinkedIn is a networking platform,

why wouldn't your network know all about how to use it and show you how with the price of your membership? If Facebook is changing to Meta and Twitter is changing to X, shouldn't our network be informed with the knowledge on how to market our businesses there? Isn't this modern networking? Traditional, old-fashioned networking models are failing us. They are not providing the course materials business owners need. It is a new age. There are now groups online that provide all kinds of training courses. We should join a group that will serve us with the knowledge we need to run a business in today's world. The membership fees we pay should include training and guidance on the most up-to-date tools so we can stop spinning our tires wasting valuable time and have the support needed to keep up with the latest in social media, software and practices.

8. **Collaboration Opportunities**. Look for a group that creates win/win/win/win situations. The collaborations of members should be good for all. The two people who are collaborating should benefit. Their clients should benefit. The networking group to which they belong should benefit. Ideally, the world should be a better place. Collaboration is not a weak JV partnership only for those with email lists. Brand new business owners and those who are new to networking should be able to put together a successful Collaboration Partnership within their first 30 days of engagement. They should be able to establish a Collaboration Pod that brings in $150,000 per year within their first three months of joining a great business network. Isn't that the kind of result you are longing for?

9. **Competition Is Low**. Collaboration brings with it a spirit of abundance. Competition brings a spirit of lack. The world is full of competitors, but a great network is a safe place. There will be others in the group who do what we do, but we should not be threatened by that. In an atmosphere of abundance, we can all be winners. Only

in a place of lack would we feel threatened. We can learn from one another where there is collaboration.

Five business coaches who all sell exactly the same thing can thrive in a collaboration climate. They will never run out of clients because of the steady stream of visitors to the network, and because of the steady stream of referrals from their collaborators, some of which would be called competitors in the old-fashioned networking model. Imagine if one business coach was losing his client after three years (which commonly happens because the client stops listening to them). Instead of saying "Goodbye," and calling it a day, he introduces that client to a competitor in his business network and refers the second coach as the expert who is needed right now. The client moves on while still being happy with his first coach and now he is ready to receive another client from one of the other coaches in his Collaboration Pod. Clients who pay for coaching always have a coach. What if we worked together to give them that coach instead of waiting for them to find someone outside of our circle? As we find the opportunities to collaborate even with competitors, the world becomes our oyster. This can only happen in a great networking organization where collaboration trumps competition every time.

10. **Giving Should Be A Key Theme**. Many networking groups talk about how the greatest givers are the biggest winners and this is true. Be sure the group we are joining is putting that theory into practice. It is not a mantra for the wall. Giving without expectation allows all involved to benefit from the gift. There is sheer joy in giving when it is done right. The giver who gives the lead wins, the person receiving the gift of the lead wins, and the referred person gets the gift of excellent service and a job well done. These are gifts to celebrate. In a great network we learn to give great referrals and we don't keep score on how many we gave. We don't keep track of the referrals that came back to us from the one guy to whom we gave a referral. We

know that sowing seed produces a crop and with that crop the seed multiplies. That one seed of corn was small and dried out, and yet powerful enough to produce. The stock of corn that grew from that seed is tall and mighty, holding cobs with thousands of kernels on each. In the same way, what we receive will look nothing like what we gave. It may not even come from the same place. It comes from the crop that is harvested and mixed into a bucket. It does not come from the one person where we gave a lead.

Gifts are not gifts if they are given with expectations. They are truly gifts if they are given in an environment where there is no immediate reciprocity expected. We cannot give a gift from our two hands extended if one hand remains out in waiting. Where is mine? This is not a gift. A great network gives good gifts to their members, and they show how to be a giver through their example. This is not something that is taught. It is caught, and you will never catch it in the old-fashioned networking model.

We have talked a lot about warm referrals and how to get them with our networking, but referrals come to people who know how to ask for them. They do come. They come naturally in an environment where the above 10 things are practiced. A great network produces professional and profitable networkers who get and give referrals.

A professionally trained networker can get warmed-up referrals from many places. We can speak with people we just met on the street, or we can set up appointments from LinkedIn with people we don't even know. We only need a strong foundation within our network where we can be trained and a tribe of like-minded people who will show us the way.

Networking is a skill, and that skill can be grown through training, practice and intent. If we are not getting the referrals we want, then there is hope. There is CIBN Connect.

Why does it matter then which network we belong to? It matters because we want to belong to a great network that is going to teach us networking skills. It matters because we should belong to a network that cares about us. We should feel we are part of a community that looks forward to seeing us every week because it can be lonely being an entrepreneur. A great network gives us support that we cannot get anywhere else. A great network offers us value on top of value. They have opportunities for valuable training that save us money because the training comes with the membership. We don't have to continually pay out of pocket for endless courses. There are several additional advantages to belonging to a great business network. One of those is we don't need to be alone in our entrepreneurial journey. With a successful team to guide us we can get to our destination faster.

Maybe reading this book has convinced you networking is awesome. Maybe you are even thinking about starting a group of your own. Perhaps yours is sadly lacking in opportunities for networking that is going to be profitable. Is it possible to start our own group? Is it even possible to start a networking organization with many groups? Running a business network without guidance is difficult. There are many mistakes one can and will make. Starting a group with the right help, however, is a great idea. Whether you want to run a group online, or start a local chapter in your city, or have a hybrid group that meets some of the time online and some of the time in person, CIBN Connect has the answers you are looking for.

CIBN Connect is the company we founded in 2012. We have help for all these things and more.

Do you know someone who is struggling to run an online group?

Do you know someone who is trying to get their in-person group to grow faster?

Do you know someone with a large Facebook group that is trying to monetize it?

Are you looking for support for the group you are trying to get off the ground?

What To Do Next

Whether you want to start business networking group, or you want to find a group that can serve you in your business, you will want to:

1. Fill out a Networking Application to join CIBN Connect as a Member here https://bit.ly/CIBNapplication

2. Attend an Introductions Meeting this week to find out more about this great network here https://cibnconnect.com/introduction-sign-up

3. Set up a Tour of the Network and have our concierge give you a bird's eye view of how it all works and be sure to ask about the Chrome Extension. It is an awesome perk that you can start using today! https://api.leadconnectorhq.com/widget/groups/bookcibn

We have the hybrid networking model that has transformed old-fashioned networking into a modern force for good. We are changing the lives of thousands of business owners every year. If you have a hunger to serve entrepreneurs in a lasting and impactful way, then this might be for you. If you want to become an influencer in your industry in this space, then reach out to us.

CIBN Connect adopts entire business organizations. We monetize large Facebook groups and we help influencers increase their bottom line.

But most of all we help individuals with their networking and their business needs. We help our members have fun while they are getting the work done. We help business owners, entrepreneurs, and professionals not just survive, but thrive, no matter the state of the economy.

We're open for business. We welcome you to come and check out this amazing business family!

> "Great salespeople are not born, they are made. We fashion ourselves into greatness through learning, training and practicing. 10,000 hours makes you an expert at anything."

> "Business owners and entrepreneurs do not think the same way. A business owner thinks in terms of percentage increase, and they still fear risk. An entrepreneur thinks in terms of multiplication and is no longer mastered by a fear of risk."

> *~Kerry George*

NETWORKING RESOURCES

- Attend an event to try out at a meeting
  https://www.thecibn.com/events

- Download the CIBN Connect Chrome Extension referral tool
  https://bit.ly/CIBNchromeXdownload or book a demo here
  https://bit.ly/CIBNchromeX

- General free networking Facebook group
  https://www.facebook.com/groups/
  networkingnetworkingnetworking

- To start a group or to monetize a group contact
  joshua@cibnconnect.com

- The general information page for networking is at
  https://cibnconnect.com/

- Business training courses can be found here
  https://cibnconnect.com/courses/

- Free training and help can be found for business owners,
  entrepreneurs, and professionals on the YouTube channel by
  searching for CIBN TV. Check out the playlists for topics that
  are of interest to those who are trying to build a business. Be
  sure to subscribe to the channel. https://bit.ly/CIBNtv

- Sales Skills. If one has been out networking without success,
  they may want to consider working on their sales skills. If
  we get twenty more leads this month and we do not have the
  ability to close those deals, then it is fruitless. The Sales Pro
  program is the membership level that helps business owners
  nail their sales and overcome the selling problem once and

for all. Lead generation will not work until one can sell. Lead generation will not work until one can sell the Sales Pro program will help you to achieve this. This is the link https://www.cibn.club/join-sales-pro-page

- Goal setting is important for business owners and it is something that needs to be done quarterly to effectively move a business forward. The Quarter Launch is a proven program that has a reputation for delivering the best results. https://www.cibn.club/quarter-launch-guests-page

- Additional courses on social media, marketing, negotiation, and sales are available to Speaker Level Members and above once they have joined the network as part of their membership packages. These are currently valued at more than $8000 and they are added to every few months. Membership starts as low as $27/month USD.

- Events to discover more https://www.thecibn.com/events

- Book a tour of the network with Joshua https://api.leadconnectorhq.com/widget/groups/bookcibn

- Membership options https://www.cibn.club/memberships-usd

Networking is making our nets work for us.

~Kerry George

THE *12* AFFIRMATIONS
OF A SUCCESSFUL NETWORKER

1. Networking is a valuable use of my time and I make time for networking.

2. I am a successful and professional networker and people are looking forward to meeting me.

3. I earn tens of thousands of dollars more through networking every year.

4. Other people from my industry have used networking to make more money; therefore, it will work for me too!

5. The people who know the people that I need to know will be at my networking meetings.

6. In the past, when networking did not seem to work for me, it was not my fault. I did not yet know what I know now.

7. I can apply what I am learning about networking to be successful at getting new clients.

8. This is the right opportunity for me to meet my revenue goals.

9. I am a hero to my family and a recognized leader in the business network to which I belong.

10. Networking is more interesting and more exciting than all of the other opportunities I have been presented with!

11. The economy is perfect for networking to work today!

12. Right now is the time to start!

The world is full of self-starters,
but what we really need is finishers.
Be a finisher. That will make you stand out.

~Kerry George

BIOGRAPHY

Kerry George is an accomplished professional networker and CEO at CIBN Connect. With over a decade of experience, she has successfully influenced and transformed the lives of entrepreneurs through her expertise in networking, masterminds, training, and consulting. Kerry's exceptional ability to bring together positive and powerful individuals has resulted in life-changing moments and significant improvements in bottom line revenue. She has an impressive track record, having facilitated thousands of networking meetings and mastermind brainstorming strategy sessions, making her highly sought after for her knowledge and insights. Kerry's focus on small businesses is commendable, as she has developed nine methods for adding $150,000 to their bottom line. CIBN Connect, under Kerry's leadership, offers unparalleled networking opportunities and sales training, making it the ideal platform for time-strapped business owners. Kerry also accepts a select number of personal consultation clients each year who have membership based businesses, ensuring their success through her no-nonsense approach and desire to get things done. With a strong work ethic, a passion for continuous learning, and a drive to add significant revenue to their businesses, clients find immense value in Kerry's mentorship. Overall, Kerry George's extensive experience, impact, and dedication to empowering entrepreneurs make her a valuable resource in the business world.

.